Lord, Teach Me How To Love

Lord, Teach Me How To Love

Learning From the Ultimate Example

by
Dr. Creflo A. Dollar Jr.

Harrison House
Tulsa, Oklahoma

Lord, Teach Me How To Love—
Learning From the Ultimate Example
ISBN 1-57794-295-7
Copyright © 2000 by Dr. Creflo A. Dollar Jr.
Creflo Dollar Ministries
P. O. Box 490124
College Park, Georgia 30349

Published by Harrison House, Inc.
P. O. Box 35035
Tulsa, Oklahoma 74153

Contents

Introduction

This is one of the most important messages I've ever taught. Just when I thought I'd found the master key to unlocking the mysteries of living a godly life, God revealed to me the ultimate master key. When revelation this deep strikes my spirit, it makes me feel like I'm getting born again all over again!

The information revealed in this book would absolutely change your life. Out of all the life-changing messages God has given me to teach over the years, I believe this one is the most important. In fact, I believe it is the most important subject in the Bible.

My study on love was a truly humbling experience. I honestly thought that I knew everything there was to know about love until God began dealing with me on a personal level about the subject. As I began to tap into this thing, I discovered a lot about love that I really didn't know. It's such a seemingly simple subject, and yet

I had not learned enough about it; neither had I taught it to God's people as I should. As a man of God, I simply couldn't bear getting to heaven only to hear God say that I failed to teach the most important subject of all—love.

Through God's divine revelation of love I reached a new level spiritually. I encourage you to open your eyes and your heart so that you might see love in a new light. As you read each chapter, ask God to reveal to you specific areas in your life where His love must be applied. I pray that through this book a conviction will come into your spirit that will make a mark in your life that can never be erased.

It is vitally important that Christians learn all there is to learn about faith, prosperity and the anointing. But without learning the true measure and meaning of love, the motivating factor behind them, we will never reach the ultimate level of God's glory here on earth.

Child of God, if you're looking for results in your life, begin to master your love walk. Challenge yourself to love others as God loves you. By spending more time in His presence, you will come to realize the meaning of His love in a truer sense. Like an eagle you will soar to new heights, and you will prosper as never before!

Transformed
by Love

Chapter 1

Transformed by Love

The church my wife, Taffi, and I pastor—World Changers Church International—began with eight members sitting around a table in an elementary school cafeteria discussing plans for the future. We didn't have much to offer the sixty people who attended our first service. There were no padded pews—only two rows of metal folding chairs. The wooden podium rocked so badly that my sermon notes would oftentimes fall off. And every now and then a rat would appear on stage.

However, in spite of the conditions, I heard the Spirit of God say, *Fill up the cafeteria with chairs. Get the members ready to receive people when I send them.* So we made everyone ushers, even though that meant there would be no one left to sit in the pews!

But something very interesting happened. Although we didn't have much to offer in the way of material comfort, there was one thing we could do—demonstrate the love of God to each visitor.

Whenever someone would come to that run-down cafeteria to attend one of our services, we would make them feel special. After the service was over, Taffi and I would ask our guests to come to the front. Then we'd thank them for coming, give them a standing ovation and hug them to let them know how much they were loved and appreciated. The change in them was immediate. I mean, the effect of God's love was written all over their faces. Their chins would rise up as if to say, *I'm special in this place. And they don't even know me!* Some were so glad to be there that they even shed tears.

After awhile Taffi and I began noticing how many of our visitors returned, and it encouraged us. We'd make every effort to speak to them and make them feel welcome. We'd say, "Brother, what's your testimony? If there's anything I can do for you, let me know. I love you, man."

It's amazing to see how much our congregation has grown over the years. Now, instead of just eight members meeting in a school cafeteria, we're more than 20,000 strong, with our meeting place completely paid for. But that only happened because from the beginning we took the responsibility of showing the love of Jesus to anyone who entered our doors.

Too Busy To Love

God's love is the kind that builds churches; however, most people tend to forget that fact after their congregation has grown larger and the church itself is more established in the community. That's when pastors and members alike become insensitive to the needs of others. The number-one concern for the hearts of people becomes obsolete in the quest to have the right image or reputation. On any given Sunday you may hear excuses like, "I don't have time to stop and pray with this person. I'll miss singing with the choir."

Oftentimes I've watched as hundreds of people pass by a man or woman walking with his or her head down, apparently needing someone to stop long enough and share the love of God with him or her. Those are the same people who, even after sitting in a church service for an hour or two, continue to walk on by wearing the title of Christian, but without the sensitivity required of one.

Someone Was Willing To Listen to Me

I grew up going to church. In fact, I was made to go to church by my mother. Her rule was very clear: "If you don't go to church, you don't go anywhere else either."

Well, you'd better believe I went to church! I even volunteered to work as a janitor, cleaning the building for thirty dollars a week. Still, in spite of all the time I spent there, something wasn't right with my life. I dabbled in all kind of things. And the whole time all I was really doing was opening myself up to demonic influences year after year. In fact, when I played football, one of the ways I would get myself psyched up was to cuss until my adrenaline levels were up.

I'll never forget the summer I realized God was trying to reach out to me. One night, I couldn't deal with hearing His voice anymore. It annoyed me. So I called one of my friends and said, "Look man, something's going on with me. I need to talk to somebody." I described to him what was happening, and he said, "Man, sounds to me like you got the exorcist in you. Bye!" I can remember even waking up in the middle of the night saying, "I'm the devil! I'm the devil!"

That same weekend a world-class track sprinter came home on vacation from the University of Alabama. We'd gone to the same high school and played sports together. So I called him up and said, "I need to talk to somebody. Something's going on with me." He said, "I know exactly what's going on with you, because I've been praying for you every day. I'll be right over."

That guy came over and told me about Jesus. Even though I'd been to church all my life, I'd never before heard any of what this friend said. He said, "Write your sins down on a piece of paper." So I did.

Then he said, "Take that piece of paper, tear it into as many pieces as you can, and throw it in the trash." After I did so, he said, "This is what happens when you ask God to forgive you and come into your life. He takes every sin, tears it into pieces, and throws it into the sea of forgetfulness. Never forget this as long as you live."

We prayed the prayer of salvation that day, and as I said those words found in Romans 10:9-10 after him and asked Jesus to come into my life, I became born again. I was so thrilled! I left that room feeling different. Something on the inside of me had changed, and there was a joy inside of me that hadn't been there before. I was finally free.

Love Kept Me Coming

A little while later, my friend said to me, "Now you have to learn how to live the life of a Christian and learn to renew your mind." So he took me to a Bible study with about twelve people in attendance.

When I walked into that apartment, all twelve people stood up to hug me and tell me how much they appreciated my being there. They welcomed me with open arms. I thought, *Man, I like the way this feels! These people love me—and they don't even know me!*

I was so excited! I could hardly wait until the next Bible study. I continued to attend because of the love demonstrated by each person there. I praise God they weren't a bunch of phonies, loving me one week and then snubbing me the next. They didn't love me because it was part of their recruitment plan. I observed their continual love for one another, and I knew they were of God.

They Will Know Us by Our Love

Jesus made it very clear in John 13:35 that the world would know us by our love: **By this shall all men know that ye are my disciples, if ye have love one to another.**

We must make it our goal to love others as God loves them. This is the only thing that draws the lost to Christ and sustains their relationship with Him—not harsh words or self-righteous attitudes.

Declare War on Complacency

I played football for a coach who once pulled me into his office and said, "I'm either going to drive you away from here or make you one of the best linebackers in the league."

I replied, "I'm man enough to take whatever you want to dish out."

You see, his words challenged me to stretch. Sometimes we need to be challenged in order to progress to the next level of maturity and spirituality. The key to your reaching that next level is learning how to love. You should not be satisfied with where you are in your walk with Christ. Never think that you have "arrived"—at least not until you get to heaven! There is always room for improvement.

It's so easy to compare ourselves to others. We see someone who is struggling in a certain area, and our tendency is to feel superior to him in some way. But that's the wrong attitude to take. There are so many areas in our lives that need improvement. We must do as Paul did in Philippians 3:12-13, and press on toward a higher level of spirituality and love.

Not as though I had already attained, either were already perfect: but I follow after, if that I may apprehend that for which also I am apprehended of Christ Jesus. Brethren, I count not myself to have apprehended: but this one thing I do, forgetting those things which are behind, and reaching forth unto those things which are before.

Opposition caused Paul to press toward His goal of knowing the fullness of God and His calling. And it was that same opposition that strengthened Paul's resolve and pushed him out of the realm of average into the realm of extraordinary.

Forget the Past

Paul said that we must forget the past—not only those things we are most ashamed of, but also those things that we are proud of. Why? Because dwelling on either one can hinder our spiritual progress and prevent us from pushing ourselves to do better. In other words, we stagnate rather than multiply.

For example, if a football player makes 15 tackles in one game, he can hardly concentrate on the next game, because in most cases, he is still dwelling on the glory of the previous tackles.

Your judgment gets clouded when you don't let go of the past. How? Because it either builds your ego or else it feeds your shame. From that point on, every decision you make will be based on one of those emotions. Paul said that spiritually mature Christians are like athletes—always pressing toward the finish line, not allowing anything to hinder them from reaching it. Our goal should be to please God in all we do. How can we do this? By showing His love to those around us. In fact, it is absolutely vital that we love with intensity.

Ask God To Fill You With Love

If you are not sure how to begin, begin by asking God to fill your heart with His love. Let Him know that you desire to see others as He does, and then go and win them to Jesus. Taffi and I did this a lot when we were dating. I remember one day we were supposed to be going to dinner, but the Lord put it on both of our hearts to knock on some apartment doors and win souls to Christ.

One guy tried to hit on Taffi. He said, "Yeah, baby, you can talk to me." She said, "You know, that's the devil in you, and that's the reason I'm here. You need to be delivered and set free!" Incredibly enough, not only was that man delivered, he accepted Christ into his heart as well. That was the best non-date Taffi and I ever had!

Don't Be Too Ashamed To Love

Maybe you're ashamed to love others, because you don't want them to think you've gone off the deep end. Or maybe it's because you feel too awkward to witness to people. However, the Bible says, **And hope maketh not ashamed; because the love of God is shed abroad in our hearts by the Holy Ghost which is given unto us** (Rom. 5:5).

When you became born again, there was a spark in your eyes that hadn't ever been there before. That was the love, presence and glory of God inside of you. All you wanted to do was share that feeling with everyone you knew. However, many people lose that sparkle with every passing year. Why? Because they forget to pour that love into the lives of those around them.

You see, God's love is magnified whenever we share it with others. God never intended for us to hoard it or cover it up.

By extending that compassion, warmth and unconditional commitment, you become more than just a person with the title of Christian. You are transformed into a true follower of Christ.

Putting First
Things First

2

Putting First Things First

Can a lack of love stop you from receiving results from God? Can Satan hinder your faith by attacking your ability to love? Can you be labeled a liar for saying you love God when you don't love others? Can you prevent God's blessings from manifesting in your life because of your unwillingness to love? The answer is yes.

You see, love is more than an emotion; it is a force. And when it is in operation it will rearrange things and change people and circumstances. The force of love is like dynamite; it's powerful and explosive in its working.

Often, the most difficult challenge is accepting the realization that love is also a decision. It's not based on a feeling. However, there is a type of love that deals with emotions and romance, which is important. But the kind of love God gives us is so much more. And when we begin to understand God's kind of love, then we'll experience the power that comes as a result of the force called love.

Obedience—God's Definition of Love

Let's look at what the Word of God tells us about love. As Christians, we know that God is love. (1 John 4:8.) And He desires that we love Him as well. But what does that kind of love require? Jesus gives us the answer in John 14:15. **If ye love me, keep my commandments.**

Obedience is the key to experiencing a true love relationship with the Father. By keeping His commandments we demonstrate our love to Him. But how can we keep His commandments if we don't know them? Now, please understand me; I'm not simply referring to the Ten Commandments, found in the book of Exodus, although they certainly must be honored. However, God has given us several guidelines to live by in His Word. And the more time we spend in His presence reading, meditating on and studying His Word, the better equipped we will become.

We can't go by what we hear in church circles. God calls us to obey His written Word, not the opinions of others. He wants us to spend time reading the Bible and to make a quality decision to do what it says. By doing so, the Word of God becomes the final authority in our lives and a mighty force in conquering the devil's attacks. How will we ever challenge the devil with the words, "It is written," if we don't know what is written? (Matt. 4:1-10.)

Child of God, it is vital for us as Christians to assemble ourselves together with other believers, studying and reading the Word in order to renew our minds. This type of obedience not only increases our love for God, but for others as well. Then we demonstrate to God that we love Him. When we do what He requires of us in His Word, we immediately communicate to all of heaven that we truly love God.

This takes us out of the emotional realm of love and centers us in the reality of God's true love. All we have to do is open the Bible like a manual or recipe book and follow the directions. That's it! God doesn't want us in church crying and falling all over the floor, moaning, "Oh God, I love You." That doesn't prove our love. The true indicator of love is *keeping His commandments!* Quite honestly, it all boils down to plain, simple obedience.

Learn To Love God First

It is vitally important that every child of God diligently cultivate a love relationship with the Father. It is very difficult to learn how to love one another if we have not yet learned how to love God. The love we show for one another comes from Him, through us and to one another. *Our horizontal relationship with one another is based on our vertical relationship with God.*

We'll talk later about the importance of developing a personal love relationship with God. But for now, understand that it is a commandment to **love the Lord thy God with all thy heart, with all thy soul, with all thy mind** (Deut. 6:5). And we demonstrate our love for the Father by doing what He tells us to do.

Some Christians love one another more than they love God. But our love for God must be first and foremost. Many people today rely on expressing their love to the Father indirectly through doing good works. "I'm going to show God I love Him by joining the usher board." Or maybe, "I'll sing in the choir." That's good, but we have to be careful not to put the cart before the horse. Jesus said the evidence of our love is in keeping God's commandments, not doing good works.

Continuing to operate in ignorance, rather than doing what God's Word says, puts us in a questionable position concerning our love toward Him. When we know what to do, but procrastinate in doing it, we operate in disobedience. For example, the Word of God says in Matthew 18:21-22 that we should forgive our neighbor seventy times seven. But if we willingly hold a grudge against that person and later forgive him, we disobey God.

The same is true when we choose to do only part of what God says. If He tells you to hug your child and tell him you're proud of him, and instead of doing so you just hug him without saying a word, you disobey God.

Partial obedience is disobedience.

Delayed obedience is disobedience.

Jesus even goes further to say we are not truly in covenant with Him if we don't obey Him.

If ye keep my commandments, ye shall abide in my love; even as I have kept my Father's commandments, and abide in his love. These things have I spoken unto you, that my joy might remain in you, and that your joy might be full.

This is my commandment, That ye love one another, as I have loved you. Greater love hath no man than this, that a man lay down his life for his friends.

Ye are my friends, if ye do whatsoever I command you.

John 15:10-14

Friend is a covenant word. Jesus basically said, "You're My friend under this condition: if you do what I tell you to do." Friendship is born out of a covenant commitment and a covenant relationship. In essence, if we fail to do what God tells us, the covenant won't produce what it said it will do. If we're to benefit from the covenant that God made with us, we have to do what He tells us to do. Otherwise we put a damper on the covenant and our friendship with God. The covenant is on the line. I don't know about you, but I want His covenant fulfilled in my life!

God is not trying to be a bully. He is trying to elevate us to His standards. He is trying to give us a better understanding of His love. He is trying to get us in position so He can do greater things in our lives. He is trying to bring us into the abundant life His Word promises.

However, God will not honor His covenant if we continue to sin by failing to do what He tells us to do. You see, sin does not just include those things we commit but also those things we *omit* or fail to do. Often, it is the things we neglect to do that result in sin.

The Bible challenges us in Hebrews 2:3 not to neglect our salvation. Many of the real problems in our lives are not from the devil. For instance, when we fail to pray, we cut short the benefits God has so freely given to us—protection, deliverance, soundness and so forth. They derive from the choices we make—the things we choose to do and not do. We must decide daily whether or not we will obey.

God is ready to give us the kingdom, but He can't give it to people who will not sit at the feet of Jesus to find out what to do. We must be willing to obey God at all cost. That's the key.

Obeying God in Our Relationships

God has given us specific instructions on how to cultivate our relationship with Him and with the people He has placed in our lives. Throughout this book, we're going to spend a great deal of time talking about relationships.

Our earthly relationships are very important to God. In fact, He essentially said that we express our love for Him by loving others: "If you don't love your brother whom you see daily, and you say you love Me, whom you have not seen, you are a liar." (1 John 4:20.)

In order to express our love to God, we must learn how to love one another without walking in envy or strife. We must have love that endures and covers with silence. We must intentionally learn how to treat one another, avoid offense and seek God for wisdom and direction in every area of our lives.

The True Measure of Love

You can say, "I love God." But where's the proof of your love? God has a system by which He measures our love for Him.

If a man say, I love God, and hateth his brother, he is a liar: for he that loveth not his brother whom he hath seen, how can he love God whom he hath not seen? And this commandment have we from him, That he who loveth God love his brother also.

1 John 4:20,21

God makes it clear that we cannot say we love Him, whom we've never seen, if we have problems with the person next to us. In other words, *to the degree that you love others, you love Him.* Jesus even said, **Inasmuch as ye have done it unto one of the least of these my brethren, ye have done it unto me** (Matt. 25:40).

How we relate with one another in the Body of Christ is vitally important to God. In fact, if we say we love God but don't love our brother, we are liars. I didn't say this—the Bible says it! We can go around and tell people how much we love the Lord, but if we're not keeping His commandments, God says we're lying.

Now, that's serious. It's easy to come to church, lift our hands and talk about how much we love God. But God sets the record straight here. He says none of that counts if we don't love one another.

Love the Whole Body of Christ

It's a poor representation in the kingdom of heaven if, from the neck down, Christians don't love one another. We just love the Head. "Ah, Jesus, we love You." We sing songs about loving the Lord, but many of us have not learned to truly love one another.

We can't say, "I'm going to love the Head portion of the body and nothing below the neck. I'll take good care of my face, but I'm not concerned about my under arms. I'll comb my hair and touch up my makeup here, but the rest will just have to do."

Christians who practice this form of preferential love, or in better terms, hypocrisy, are often the biggest turn-off to unbelievers. They are a poor representation of the Body of Christ, and many unbelievers are convinced we're all the same.

One reason for that attitude is the way church folk act. They claim to love God, yet people hear them gossiping, being cruel to one another, backbiting. So people figure, *I don't want to get involved in that, so I'm just going to tend to my own business.*

It's sad that it's come to that. It's sad that people would rather come to church, hear the Word and get out as quickly as they can so they can avoid direct contact with church folk! Until we straighten out the relationships we have with the people we see every day, we can't say that we love God, whom we've never seen!

We have to deal with these issues, because the Bible requires us to walk in love one with another. Remember, if I don't get my love life corrected and if I don't start walking in the love of God, then according to His Word, in heaven's eye, I am a useless nobody. (1 Cor. 13:2 AMP.)

Think about all that you're doing for God. Think about the choir and all the activities. But none of that matters. Until you allow the love of God to begin operating in your life, you are a useless nobody.

On the other hand, you might not be able to sing a note, and you might not be able to interpret every tongue you hear, and you might not be able to heal everybody that's sick. But as long as you have love, God will find a way to use you.

Until we let go of the grudges we hold against people who've hurt us, we can't say we love God. We still have a problem with daddy—and he's dead now. We still have a problem with that ex-husband or that ex-wife. We still have a problem with the pastor of the church we went to twenty years ago! We have a lot of unresolved issues, a lot of dead skeletons lingering in the closet.

The church has congregations of people who have been hurt, abused, persecuted, lied to and talked about. Yet the thing that should distinguish us from the world is our love for one another. Jesus said, **By this shall all men know that ye are my disciples, if ye have love one to another** (John 13:35).

I've taught my church leaders what I believe is the most important aspect of leadership: not to get so busy leading people that we forget to love them. And the thing we have to lead people into more than anything else is the love walk. We need to deal with the love issue over and over again, until an epidemic starts. And just as people catch colds, we'll catch this love bug!

Anointed To Love

Chapter 3

Anointed To Love

When we consistently operate in the love of God, we walk in the fullness of His power. However, when we are not rooted in His love it short-circuits our relationship with God, therefore hindering His ability to work in our lives.

For this cause I bow my knees unto the Father of our Lord Jesus Christ, of whom the whole family in heaven and earth is named, that he would grant you, according to the riches of his glory, to be strengthened with might by his Spirit in the inner man; that Christ may dwell in your hearts by faith; that ye, being rooted and grounded in love, may be able to comprehend with all saints what is the breadth, and length, and depth, and height; and to know the love of Christ, which passeth knowledge, that ye might be filled with all the fulness of God.

Ephesians 3:14-19

God wants to strengthen us with His might—the ability to do anything. However, this can only happen when we become rooted and grounded in His love. Look at it this way—whatever fruit we bear in our lives is determined by our roots.

For example, a healthy, well-watered tree bears good fruit, while a decayed, malnourished tree doesn't bear fruit at all. Likewise, as the roots of a plant draw nourishment from the soil, our hearts and minds draw nourishment from our heavenly Father. By planting yourself firmly in God's love, you bear the fruit of His Spirit almost effortlessly. However, if you are rooted in the world, your fruit will be almost nonexistent. Why? Because only God's love can give us everything we need for victorious Christian living. Faith can't be our root. The anointing can't be our root. Only the fruit that comes from being grounded in His love can produce positive, God-like results.

Take a look at your roots. If you find your love roots are nonexistent or rotten, you will understand why miraculous things haven't happened in your life. God's miracle-working power is His anointing—God's burden-removing, yoke-destroying power, revealed in Isaiah 61:1.

When we become rooted and grounded in God's love, His power is released in our lives. That's when we can say to our mountains of debt, sickness and divorce, "Be thou removed" (Mark 11:23), and then watch them disappear.

The Bible Reveals God's Love

The Bible is not a revelation of God's power; instead, it is a revelation of His love. And when we dig into His Word and begin to truly understand all the aspects of His love, we'll begin tapping into His awesome power.

Many Christians struggle with a lot of things because they are not rooted and grounded in love. They have yet to comprehend the breadth, length, depth and height of it. They miss out on a great deal because God talks to and works through us out of the love relationship we have established with Him through His Son, Jesus Christ. In other words, He speaks regularly to those who are rooted and grounded in Him.

When we're rooted and grounded in God's love, our compassion and concern for others is at the forefront of our thinking. That's when God's power works through us in order to minister to them. Too many of us search for power instead of love. We say, "Give me power, Lord! Power! Wonder-working power!" And God says, "OK, let me teach you how to love—and then you'll have power!" You see, the power is not going to show up until the love shows up. It's impossible to receive one without the other. Remember, God is love. And nothing on earth is more powerful than Him.

God's Love Precedes His Power

Let me paint a picture of Jesus so you can emotionally experience what He experienced. Then you will better understand how His compassion led to the manifestation of His power.

But when Herod's birthday was kept, the daughter of Herodias danced before them, and pleased Herod. Whereupon he promised with an oath to give her whatsoever she would ask.

And she, being before instructed of her mother, said, Give me here John Baptist's head in a charger.

And the king was sorry: nevertheless for the oath's sake, and them which sat with him at meat, he commanded it to be given her. And he sent, and beheaded John in the prison. And his head was brought in a charger, and given to the damsel: and she brought it to her mother.

And his disciples came, and took up the body, and buried it, and went and told Jesus.

Matthew 14:6-12

Herodias' daughter danced before Herod and seduced him until he was consumed with lust. After the whole thing was over, she told him, "You said I could have anything I asked for. I want the head of John the Baptist on a platter." So John's head was cut off because of a stupid oath Herod made while in lust.

John the Baptist was Jesus' first cousin. Put yourself in Jesus' position. You've just heard that your first cousin was beheaded and that the Romans are parading it around the city. Now, I don't care how saved you are—that does something to your emotions!

Wouldn't you want to do something about it if your cousin were treated this way? Wouldn't you want to take revenge? Jesus had the power to call down legions of angels. One word from Him, and Herod would've found himself on the other side of eternity. But look at what Jesus did instead:

When Jesus heard of it, he departed thence by ship into a desert place apart: and when the people had heard thereof, they followed him on foot out of the cities.

*And Jesus went forth, and saw a great multitude, **and was moved with compassion** toward them, and He healed their sick.*

Matthew 14:13,14

When Jesus heard of His cousin's murder, He took some time to be alone. Personally, I believe He went to pray and get His emotions under control. However, when the crowd heard of His departure, they followed Him. My first thought would've been, *How insensitive! Just leave me alone!*

But when Jesus looked at the people, He saw a group that was hungry for food and for His anointing. He saw their need, and compassion moved Him to heal their diseases. In other words, Jesus prayed, and the healing power manifested itself.

Prayer. Compassion. Power. That's the formula for producing the God-kind of love. First we see Jesus spending time alone with His Father; then we see Him being filled with the Father's compassion. Finally we see the Father manifesting His power through Jesus by healing the sick. Now look at it from a different angle. First we see vertical love between Jesus and the Father. Next we see horizontal love from Jesus to the people. Then we see God's power at work.

Do you want power? Do you want anointing? Do you want to see lives changed? Do you want to see the sick healed and made whole? Then go to the Father, and get filled with His love first!

Prayer connects us to God and establishes our love relationship with Him; as a result, compassion is developed within us and is brought forth. When we allow the love of God to move us with compassion toward others, God can display His power through us. However, our motivation for displaying His power must be sincere compassion to see others saved, delivered and healed, rather than for earthly praise and recognition.

What moves you to feed the hungry? What moves you to witness to the lost? Are you motivated by lust and selfish gain or by love? Lust is a strong, unquenchable desire for something. It never gets enough. Instead, lust takes as much as it can without giving anything in return.

Now's a good time to do a reality check. What motivates you— power, praise or God? Judge yourself carefully.

Jesus Was Moved With Compassion

I'll never forget what Oral Roberts once told me. He said, "Son, you'll never see the power of healing operate in your ministry until you first see Jesus."

I didn't know what he was talking about then, but I know now. See, compassion flows from the deepest part of a person. When I understood Jesus' compassion, I saw Him. And when I saw Him and His compassion, the ministry of healing began to take off in my life. That's because when I'm moved with Jesus' compassion, God reveals His power through me.

But that power is not to make me look good. Actually, manifestations like healing should draw our focus to God, because it's a demonstration of His compassion. The love of God is not selfish, arrogant or prideful. The love of God says, "What can I do for *you?*" It constantly gives.

I've heard many say, "If you pray, you'll receive power." You know, that may help, but if you turn prayer into a mechanical thing and pray without love or compassion, you won't be operating to the fullest capacity of God's power. I don't know about you, but I don't want to be powerless in this life! I want my life to be full of God's power. It's like baseball. I can't skip first base and try to get to home plate, or the umpire will say that I'm out. I can touch second, third and home plate, but if I still miss first base, I'm out.

God said, **Bear ye one another's burdens** (Gal. 6:2). That means your thinking should be, *I love others with the love of God. I want so much for their lives to be changed. I want so much for their bodies to be healed. Oh God, help me to help them!* And the Lord will allow His anointing to flow through your life. Whether it's counsel, might, wisdom or money, it will come when God's love begins operating in your life. Remember, love produces power, and power produces the anointing.

Jesus has called us to walk in love. His is the kind of love that causes us to respond positively even when watching negative reports on a newscast, for example. We may say, "God, what can I do to help in this situation? That child was abandoned." Or "This family's house burned down. What can I do?"

There are needs that God desires to meet through your hands. There are things He wants to do through you. But He can't use you if you don't know how to love. He can't work through you if you're just concerned about the mechanics of ministry and disinterested in the heartbeat of ministry—loving His people.

We're Useless Without Love

God is so intent on our learning to love that He says if we don't love, we're useless.

If I [can] speak in the tongues of men and [even] of angels, but have not love [that reasoning, intentional, spiritual devotion such as is inspired by God's love for and in us], I am only a noisy gong or a clanging cymbal.

And if I have prophetic powers (the gift of interpreting the divine will and purpose), and understand all the secret truths and mysteries and possess all knowledge, and if I have [sufficient] faith so that I can remove mountains, but have not love (God's love in me) I am nothing (a useless nobody).

Even if I dole out all that I have [to the poor in providing] food, and if I surrender my body to be burned or in order that I may glory, but have not love (God's love in me), I gain nothing.

1 Corinthians 13:1-3 AMP

Amen

Good works cannot be substituted for the love of God, because good works without love are empty. They don't amount to anything. We can do a lot of noble things, like feeding the hungry and visiting the sick; however, none of those things will truly profit anyone if our actions aren't motivated by love.

We can speak in tongues for two and three hours a day; but if we don't have love in our hearts, what's the point of praying? I mean, we've got to be willing to put the needs of others first in our prayers. Otherwise we're just making a lot of noise!

The Bible says we can operate in the gifts of the Spirit and have the anointing to prophesy, interpret tongues and lay hands on the sick. We can even understand mysteries, interpret dreams and have revelation knowledge. Yet, this passage says, **If I have [sufficient] faith so that I can remove mountains, but have**

not love (God's love in me) I am nothing (a useless nobody)

(1 Cor. 13:2 AMP). I don't know about you, but I have no intention of being a useless nobody—not on earth or in heaven!

Someone may be thinking, *When I get to heaven, they're going to put so many crowns on me that my head is going to tilt from all the weight.* However, if you don't have love, all of heaven considers you nothing more than a useless nobody.

I'll tell you one thing, that phrase *useless nobody* gets my attention! I can preach messages that stir souls, and I can pack convention centers all around the world; but if I don't have love, I am a useless nobody.

We need to take some of the time and effort we put into other areas of our lives and put them into our love walk. It is our love for others that will make us somebodies in heaven.

Learn To Love Unconditionally

Have you ever loved someone based on how he or she treated you? That's called conditional love. But God's love is unconditional. No matter how you treat Him, His love remains the same. That's how He wants us to be.

Every time we walk through the door, someone's depression should lift and another's concerns minimize because they've encountered God's love and power at work in us. It might just be one little hug, an "I really appreciate you" or an "I'm concerned about you" that could change their lives forever.

My wife, Taffi, and I are committed to making our church an oasis of love. More than knowledge, understanding, healing or prosperity, we're learning about *love* by practicing God's Word. And when our congregation settles this love issue, a lot of other issues will be settled simultaneously.

Everyone Can Love

You might not have great faith, but you can love! You might not be able to prophesy, but you can love! You may not have the gift of interpretation of tongues, but you can love! You may not be able to preach a soul-stirring sermon, but everybody—from the youngest to the oldest, from the least to the greatest—has the capacity to operate in love.

The Power
of Love

Chapter 4

The Power of Love

Everything in the kingdom of God operates by faith. This includes healing, deliverance and prosperity. The Bible refers to faith as the key to unlocking whatever resources we need or desire. It brings them from the spiritual realm to the natural realm.

Faith coupled with the Word of God can produce awesome results. By faith we believe, act on and consistently speak the Word over our circumstances. By faith we also believe we are who the Bible says we are and can do what it says we can do. Through faith we make the Word our final authority by speaking it, hearing it, meditating on it and acting on it.

Faith Works by Love

Have you ever wondered why your prayers were unanswered? Or why you didn't receive a breakthrough after applying the principles you learned in church? I certainly have. So I began to search the Scriptures for answers and made an awesome discovery!

For we through the Spirit wait for the hope of righteousness by faith. For in Jesus Christ neither circumcision availeth any thing, nor uncircumcision; but faith which worketh by love.

Galatians 5:5,6

Faith works by love!

Even though faith is activated by our confessions, it only actually works when we apply love. And yet many people have neither seen nor experienced the manifestation of their faith. You see, you can have a flashlight, but until you put batteries in it, that flashlight won't work. Love is like that battery. Everything in the kingdom of God operates by faith, but faith won't work without love.

Think about some of the things you've been believing God for. It may be getting out of debt, getting a promotion or receiving your healing. You may have been praying about those things for weeks, months or even years—and still no answer from God.

Well, that's not the kind of God we serve. In 3 John 2 God reveals His desire for us: **Beloved, I wish above all things, that thou mayest prosper and be in health, even as thy soul prospereth.**

Therefore, if God is willing to give us His best, there must be a missing element on our end. How are your relationships fairing these days? Maybe you're having problems with just one; however, that could be the very thing hindering your blessings. The Bible says that our faith won't work if our love is not working.

When we are rooted and grounded in God's love, our faith ignites His power. But when our love generators are damaged or no longer operating because of offense, unforgiveness or disobedience, we can't expect the manifestation of our prayers.

I don't have to struggle anymore with the question, "Oh God, why aren't you answering my prayers?" I know if my faith is not working, it's because my love is not working.

Faith is active. It will change things. It will move mountains. But faith that's not backed up by love is powerless, because *faith works by love.* Love is the force behind faith. It's explosive and active; it causes great things to happen. So if your faith runs out of gas and stops moving, go fill up your tank with premium love and watch your faith work as never before.

No Fear in Love

Another great hindrance to our faith is fear. Romans 10:17 says, **Faith cometh by hearing, and hearing by the word of God.** Conversely, fear comes by hearing the words of the devil. What we hear will either produce faith or fear. And when fear is sown, it produces a harvest of torment in our lives. The Bible teaches us how to get rid of fear.

There is no fear in love; but perfect love casteth out fear: because fear hath torment. He that feareth is not made perfect in love.

1 John 4:18

Here again we see the power of love in action. Love ignites faith while extinguishing fear.

Remember, perfect love is doing what the Father tells us to do. When we're obedient to the commandment, **Love the Lord thy God with all thy heart, with all thy soul, with all thy might** (Deut. 6:5), we activate our faith and dispel fear. **God hath not given us the spirit of fear; but of power, and of love, and of a sound mind** (2 Tim. 1:7). When we realize that God is with us and His Word is true, fear disappears.

Fear brings torment and ultimately produces dread. When we fear something, we dread doing it. But God says in 1 John 4:18 that walking in perfect love will remove the apprehension, dread and fear.

The more time we spend developing a relationship with God, the less time we'll spend operating in fear. When we exercise our love for God by doing what He tells us to do, fear leaves our lives. In other words, when we cultivate love for the Father, we walk in absence of fear.

Just as God uses faith to bring His words to pass, Satan uses fear to bring his words to pass. Fear is the "faith" of the devil. The Bible says if we meditate on the Word day and night we'll make our way prosperous and have good success. (Josh. 1:8.) Whereas, if we worry over the devil's words day and night, we will only be successful in seeing the manifestation of fear and worry come to pass. (Job 3:25.)

Worry is nothing more than a negative form of meditation. When we worry, we ponder negative thoughts over and over again, and they create destruction and torment in our lives. The Bible says we are to cast our care on God because He cares for us. (1 Peter 5:7.) But when we worry, we are essentially saying, "I don't need you right now, God. I can take care of myself."

When we do that, we become god over our own lives. Scripture confirms in Jeremiah 32:17 that there is nothing too hard for God. We must learn to allow God to handle our circumstances. He can do much more than we ever could.

As the old song goes, *"Take your burdens to the Lord and leave them there."*[1] However, leaving them there is the problem for many of us. How many times have you given your burdens to the Lord, either at the altar or in prayer, experienced temporary relief and then suddenly become overwhelmed by the circumstance all over again?

Worry and fear are cancers that try to destroy you from the inside out. Satan uses fear and worry as weapons to torment us. When you allow yourself to meditate on negative thoughts, you are cooperating with the devil's plans. Think about it. The things you generally meditate on are the things that eventually happen. That's why God admonishes us to occupy our minds with good things.

Finally, brethren, whatsoever things are true, whatsoever things are honest, whatsoever things are just, whatsoever things are pure, whatsoever things are lovely, whatsoever things are of good report; if there be any virtue, and if there be any praise, think on these things.... And the God of peace shall be with you.

Philippians 4:8,9

Don't Settle for Fear

Many people today are apprehensive about the future. The Father warned us about this increasing fear and the dangers associated with it.

Men swooning away or expiring with fear and dread and apprehension and expectation of the things that are coming on the world; for the [very] powers of the heaven will be shaken and caused to totter.

Luke 21:26 AMP

No matter what evil reports the media, economists or doctors give us, we must choose to walk in confidence rather than fear. We do not settle for fear, because we remember, "God is with me." We say, **"The Lord is my helper; I will not fear. What can man do to me?"** (Heb. 13:6 NKJV). We talk to Him every day. We're in love with Him, and we know He is in love with us and won't let anything happen to us. Jesus said:

Are not two sparrows sold for a farthing? and one of them shall not fall on the ground without your Father. But the very hairs of your head are all numbered. Fear ye not therefore, ye are of more value than many sparrows.

Matthew 10:29-31

If we fully realized our Father's infinite power and love for us, we would no longer walk in fear. God is the One who created us. He is aware of everything going on with us. He is so aware of who we are that He even knows the number of hairs on our heads.

Now, some people think that because God is aware of them, He will take responsibility for them. But being aware of them and being responsible for what's going on with them are two different things.

Yes, He's aware of the situation. Yes, He's aware of the problem. But He's also aware of what they've done to cause the harvest of that problem to come into their lives. The Bible says our harvest is based on the seeds we sow. If we don't like our harvest, we need to change the seed. Nothing just happens. No, usually something we've done or are doing causes it to happen.

If we'll cultivate our love relationship with God, He can help identify what the problems are. If we'll pray and open ourselves up to fellowshipping with God, He can help us out of our dilemmas. He's aware of what we need to do. He knows the way out.

Give Him a Way Into Your Life—Pray

But unless we give Him a way into our lives, God will not be able to show us the way out of our dilemmas. He asks, *Can I please talk to you?* But we say, "Lord, I'm too busy. I've got to work in the children's ministry." He responds, *I'm aware that you're in a sticky situation.* We reply, "Yeah, I know I'm in a sticky situation, Lord, but I can't talk to You now. I've got to hurry up and get to choir rehearsal."

Some people's prayer lives have become nonexistent. They go to bed, get up and they don't even pray. Some Christians pray like there's no tomorrow, but others act like prayer is a foreign word.

The most anointed men and women in the world all have this one thing in common: They know how to practice the presence of God. They know how to talk to God when they are in their cars. They know how to talk to God when they are at home. They know how to turn off the television and say, "Jesus, let's talk." They know how to listen to God, and they have confidence that when they pray, God hears and answers them.

Spending time with God and His Word should be our number-one priority. When this happens, everything in our lives will flow in prosperity, increase and victory.

God wants us to pray. He yearns to be involved in our lives.

For he hath said, I will never leave thee, nor forsake thee. So that we may boldly say, The Lord is my helper.

Hebrews 13:5,6

When we enter into a love relationship with our Father through prayer, we can shout out, "The Lord is my helper!" every time a problem arises. Whenever the doctor tells us about some ailment in our bodies that we didn't know about, we can shout out, "God is my helper, and I will not fear."

God's Love Is the Answer

You see, love is the antidote to fear, and it is the foundation of faith. Thank God for faith conventions, faith seminars, the five steps of faith and the two steps to the highest kind of faith. But we may as well forget all those things if we haven't learned this love step. Everything in the Bible works by love!

Throughout the years, love has been considered an insignificant subject. But the lack of love is the very thing that's stopping us from getting results in our lives. We don't know how to love our spouses. We don't know how to love our children. We don't even know how to love our God. And we certainly don't know how to love our fellow man, because we haven't learned what the Word of God says about love.

We need to find out how to love according to the Word so we'll do it properly, so our faith will work, so the power can come, so Satan can be defeated. When we're walking in the love of God, it produces everything necessary for us to win in every area of our lives. Where there's a place of love, there's also a place of power.

We can talk about prosperity until we're blue in the face, but if we're failing in the love walk, none of the laws of prosperity will work, because they're being cut off. We can sow. We can tithe. We can give first fruits. We can declare, "I'm out of debt. My needs are met. I've got plenty more to put in store." We can do all those things—and they're wonderful—but without love, they won't work.

Our confessions don't work, because our love is not working. We're trying to get out of debt, but our love is not working. We've been working for twenty-five years and haven't received a promotion yet. We wonder why the Lord won't hear our prayers, but our love is not working. We open up our mouths and make confession after confession after confession. We say them fifty times a day. We obligate Jesus and the angels—and yet, without love, none of it comes to pass.

Love Backs Up Our Faith

Love backs up our confessions of faith, which activate the things of God's Word. Here's a story that illustrates what I mean.

When I went home yesterday, it was hot in my house. I thought, *It's not supposed to be hot in here.* I put my hand by the vent and felt some air, but not much. I thought, *Something's wrong.* I went outside and looked at the air conditioning unit, and the motor in the fan wasn't running. The air was trying to blow, but the motor wasn't backing it up. So all I got was heat.

You know, some of our lives are like that. We let out a lot of hot air. We say a lot of things and do a lot of things, but if the motor (love) is not running, the climate won't change—we won't receive our answer.

What Is Your Motivation?

Love, not lust, must be the motivation behind our faith. Some of us have a wrong relationship with material things, which hinders our prosperity. That was the problem the children of Israel had when they were trying to possess the Promised Land. They had so many issues, so much baggage. They couldn't enter into the Promised Land because God couldn't trust them in their arrogance and ingratitude. He knew they'd forget about Him once they got there.

Faith is required to lay hold of and receive whatever it is we're trying to receive; but if our love is not working, then our faith isn't working. We'll still be in the same situation and circumstance, even though we've declared the answer from the Word with our mouths.

Look at a couple of biblical examples about the correlation between love and prosperity.

Let's look first at Matthew 14. After the death of His first cousin John broke Jesus' heart, He saw that the multitude who followed Him were hungry. So He said to His disciples, "Bring Me the two-piece fish dinner." Why? Because He loved them. Jesus basically said, "As an act of My love, I'm going to show you My power. Because I love this multitude, watch what I do with this two-piece fish dinner. My love is so strong for them that the power has to show up. Something has to happen because I love them."

And he commanded the multitude to sit down on the grass, and took the five loaves, and the two fishes, and looking up to heaven, he blessed, and brake, and gave the loaves to his disciples, and the disciples to the multitude.

Matthew 14:19

To *bless* means to empower to prosper.[2] Jesus empowered the two-piece fish dinner to prosper. He anointed that dinner to feed over 20,000 people—and 20,000 hungry people is a burden and a yoke. But the anointing removes burdens and destroys yokes.

Lack is a burden. Shortage is a burden. But when the anointing gets on that lack and shortage, it does something about them, and we receive a harvest!

Thank God we get a harvest when we sow; but remember, God's acts are not due to our obedience as much as they are simply an expression of love from a Father who cares for us! That's why the system works. God supports the system He set into motion with His love.

Love Produces Power and Prosperity

God makes His power available for everybody, but who will decide to tap into that power by tapping into a relationship of love with the Father and with the people around them?

Now let's look in 1 Samuel to see another biblical example of the correlation between love and prosperity. David was a teenager who obeyed God by spending time with Him. When he was presented with the opportunity to make his whole family free of debt, marry the king's daughter and get her inheritance by killing Goliath the giant, he couldn't understand why anyone wouldn't accept the challenge.

So he said, "Who is this uncircumcised Philistine who doesn't even have a covenant with God? I killed a lion and a bear by standing on this covenant. I knew that lion couldn't mess with me, because God loves me. And because I know God loves me, I'm going to bring this big Philistine down." (1 Sam. 17:26,34-37.)

So because David was confident in God's love for Him, he faced that giant, and God empowered him to kill Goliath. As a result, wealth was transferred to him in abundance.

Check Your Battery

Can you imagine at age seventeen getting your parents out of debt? Is it hard for you to imagine getting yourself out of debt now? Maybe you're believing God for a promotion and it hasn't come yet. Or maybe you're believing God for healing or for restoration in your marriage or family and it hasn't come yet.

You've been busily looking over the faith steps you've been taking and have increased your confessions, but maybe that's not the area you should be examining. Maybe the area you should be looking at very closely is that battery called love, because faith won't work without the batteries.

We may understand the prosperity message. But if we get all the worldly goods and still don't have love, it's all worthless. Only when we are rooted and grounded in the love of God, only when we love God and love one another and only when we keep God's commandments will God bring us to the harvest of our dreams and desires.

And you have invested too much time, too much prayer and too much money not to get that harvest!

The Nature
of Love

Chapter 5

The Nature of Love

Faith works by love. (Gal. 5:6.) In other words, love employs our faith. The devil understands how lethal faith is to his plans. So in an effort to stop our faith, he attacks our love with the weapon of anger. If he can distract us, he can short-circuit our faith.

Every time we reach out to take revenge or gossip, we sow seeds that hurt ourselves. Because love is not in operation, faith is hindered. Well, I don't know about you, but I have too much seed in the ground to be mad at somebody and lose my harvest! But I'm warning you, the more you learn about love, the more you'll be challenged in this area. I was challenged when I least expected it.

As I was preparing a series of teachings on love, my son and I went to a neighborhood sandwich shop. I told him, "Go ahead and order for me while I sit." But when I stood up to pay, the clerk looked at me and said, "Ooh, you're stuck up! The Bible said, thou shall not be stuck up!" I hadn't even said a thing to her! My study on love almost went out the window!

So we sat down and ate our sandwiches, but the clerk came out from behind the counter and said, "I want you to know there's going to be a bomb threat in about twenty-five minutes, so hurry up." And I'm thinking, *Lord, is this a test?* Then she came back and commanded, "You make sure you clean up! Don't you leave a mess here!" I knew I had to walk in love, but I thought, *No more sandwich shop! It's time to go!*

As we begin perfecting our love walk, Satan will use people we don't even know to drain our reserves in order to stop our faith from working. That's when we need to just get up and leave. Don't sit there and try to take it! The more we strive to walk in love, the more our love will be challenged in our relationships with everyone around us.

Are you guilty of making statements like these? "That person in the parking lot makes me sick!" Or, "That person in the choir gets on my nerves!" If so, you need to improve your love walk. How we treat one another is extremely important to God. When we obey God's commandment to love one another, it forces us to confront the sticky issues in our lives. We can no longer continue living with unforgiveness, strife, envy and jealousy, because if we say we love God yet have hatred toward our brothers in Christ, then we are liars.

Ask yourself, *Am I a Christian, or am I religious?* You see, if you're religious you'll be willing to help pass out food boxes and go soul-winning, but you probably won't be as willing to make the first steps toward loving your enemy. Religion often tries to get the attention of men to win the title of "Good Samaritan."

It doesn't mean a thing to come to church all the time if you're not willing to work out misunderstandings, mend broken relationships and love even when it's difficult to do so. True Christianity is walking in love to the point that every time others are around us, they are somehow positively affected by our genuine love.

God's Description of Love

In 1 Corinthians 13:4-5, Paul defines love.

Love endures long and is patient and kind; love never is envious nor boils over with jealousy, is not boastful or vainglorious, does not display itself haughtily.

It is not conceited (arrogant and inflated with pride); it is not rude (unmannerly) and does not act unbecomingly. Love (God's love in us) does not insist on its own rights or its own way, for it is not self-seeking; it is not touchy or fretful or resentful; it takes no account of the evil done to it [it pays no attention to a suffered wrong].

1 Corinthians 13:4,5 AMP

Love Endures Long

When we talk about loving one another, the first thing we have to be aware of is that love is for the long haul. Love is not the forty-yard dash. Love is the marathon. The love of God endures no matter what comes along—regardless of the inconsistencies and imperfections in our lives. The love of God says, "You keep messing up and falling down, but I'm going to keep loving you." The love of God will always outlast our sinful nature.

God has unconditional love for us; however, the church is notorious for operating in conditional love. We are so quick to give up on people. We say we love them, but we generally operate by the love that says, "I'll love you as long as you keep pleasing me. As soon as you disappoint or anger me or fall in sin, I'm out of here." But God's love endures. It outlasts any problem that may come your way.

Now, it's true that there are instances in the Bible in which we're told not to even eat with a brother caught up in sin (1 Cor. 5:11.) In this case, the Scripture is referring to someone who has been shown his error through the Word of God and defiantly refuses to change. When someone shows an outright disregard for God's Word, he should be left alone to consider his thoughts and actions. If we don't leave him alone, he won't be able to see that he's wrong. In other words, it may jeopardize his chances of coming back to God.

But just because we cut off our fellowship with such people doesn't mean we cut off our love for them. It simply means that for now it is appropriate that we love them from a distance. Often, during this time of separation, God performs miraculous surgery. As soon as they see they're wrong and are willing to do right, we are to be the first to extend our arms and say, "I never stopped loving you. I've been waiting on you the whole time!"

There have been people in my life that I have determined to love supernaturally. They may act crazy, but I love them and keep loving them anyway. And after they are finished acting crazy, I'll still be there loving them.

That's the kind of love God wants us to have because He did the same for us before we came to know Him. God loved us in the midst of our foolishness. You may have been smoking marijuana, sleeping with multiple partners and partying all the time, but God said, *I'm not going to allow your mess to outlast My love.* That's why we can't leave Him. Every time we think about backsliding, we should recall how God loved us even when we didn't deserve His love. The Bible says the goodness of God brings a man to repentance: **Despisest thou the riches of his goodness and forbearance and longsuffering; not knowing that the goodness of God leadeth thee to repentance?** (Rom. 2:4). In other words, the goodness of God causes a man to change.

How much endurance does your love have? Are you ready to divorce your spouse at the first sign of trouble? Are you ready to cut off the friend who said something to hurt your feelings? How much will your love outlast?

Love Is Patient

Patience doesn't mean to put up with something. Instead, it means "constancy; continuance."[1] If you apply patience to your faith, it means you are constant in your belief in the Word of God. If you understand God to be the healer, then you believe He is the healer before, during and after an attack on your body. The Word of God says:

And not only so, but we glory in tribulations also: knowing that tribulation worketh patience.

Romans 5:3

Read this correctly. Tribulation does *not* produce patience. If trouble produced patience, we would be the most patient people alive, simply because we're not lacking trouble. *Worketh* means to employ, as an employer employs someone.[2] In other words, when tribulation is on the scene, what should you hire? Patience. When trouble arises, patience comes to the rescue. That means we just keep believing God's Word and pressing through.

We must love others when we first meet them, when they mess up and after they've straightened out. Love motivates us to be patient. Even when everyone says so-and-so is not going to make it, we hang in there with him and as a result, we get the joy of seeing him come through.

Love Is Never Envious

When we truly love someone, we do not envy him. Envy is something that a lot of people don't want to admit they have. The best way to identify envy in your life is to see how you react when somebody is promoted or blessed. If you experience discomfort or ill will, then you are guilty of harboring envy in your heart. For example, when someone gets a new house, an envious person says, "When is the Lord going to bless *me?*" or, "That house isn't that great. I don't know why you keep talking about it like it's a mansion."

One reason we are not able to move up ourselves is that envy keeps us right where we are. Instead of rejoicing, we're envious. But when we truly love others, it gives us great joy to see the blessings and promotion of God manifest in their lives. The Bible says, **Rejoice with them that do rejoice** (Rom. 12:15). When you're filled with God's love, you rejoice: "I'm so glad you got that house. Man, God really answers prayers! Thank You, Jesus!"

We should be glad when people we know receive blessings, because that means the line is moving and we're that much closer to getting ours. But some of us are just so stubborn that we refuse to rejoice. We look at people and get envious of them. If it doesn't happen to us, we're mad at the world. Perhaps one of the reasons some people are still in debt today is that they wouldn't rejoice with the person who got a promotion last year.

Child of God, get delivered! You can't afford to envy anyone. God said to *rejoice,* so rejoice and be exceedingly glad.

Love Never Boils Over With Jealousy

Many people don't realize it, but one of the most harmful effects of becoming jealous is that it cuts the very life out of our prayers.

Jealousy leads us to murmuring and complaining. As a result, we hinder the anointing and the manifestation of our blessings. When we become jealous of someone's marital relationship or look at someone who has something we don't have and respond with jealousy rather than joy, we limit ourselves.

Jealousy is always motivated by lack. Many times we respond to other people's blessings by trying to hurt them. Our insecurities motivate us to lash out in order to make us feel better about not having something. But what we're really doing is hindering our own blessings.

True love says, "I love you, and I appreciate all that God is doing in your life." This kind of love opens the door to our blessing.

Love Is Not Proud

When God invests in our lives, He intends to get the glory. He taught Israel about this. He pointed out to them that they were taking the credit for the wealth they had. But God said, "No, I'm the One giving you the power to get the wealth." (Deut. 8:18.)

God wants us to give Him the glory when we are blessed, promoted and delivered. By doing so, we avoid being arrogant, conceited and puffed up.

The Bible says a proud look is one of the things He hates more than anything. (Prov. 6:16,17.) God has a problem with people who are always boasting about their accomplishments. Every time you fellowship with them, they want to talk about what they have done and what they bought. They tell you, "Oh, you ain't seen nothing until you've seen mine!"

Wait a minute! God wants to make sure that when people hear about your blessings, He gets the glory. People come to church with strife, arrogance, pride and haughty looks. They're puffed up because they get blessed more than others or they grow more spiritually than others. That proud look says, "I did it all myself. I am my own god. I did it my way."

Anywhere you see the spirit of "I," you see the spirit of Satan. He said, *I will ascend into heaven, I will exalt my throne above the stars of God.... I will be like the most High* (Isa. 14:13,14). And he still wants to do this today—through you!

Instead of bragging on ourselves, we should be bragging on our God. When we do this, we'll become witnesses to God's power and supernatural abundance. Instead of grumbling and complaining, we'll be able to say, "Did you see what the Lord did? Look at how He honored His Word."

We didn't do it by ourselves. The reason we're blessed is that God loves us so much. Give Him glory for the car! The house! The job! Talk like this: "If it had not been for the Lord on my side, I don't know how we would have had the idea. And once we had the idea, if it had not been for the Lord, I don't know how the money would have come. And even when the money got here, we needed wisdom to put the plan together. And the Lord showed up in the midnight hour and gave us the solution in a dream. It was God who prospered us!"

Anytime you think you did something yourself, remember what God said to Job. He said, in essence, "Job, tell Me how I hung the stars in the sky. Explain to Me why the water comes up on the beach and returns exactly when it should. If you know so much, explain to Me how the earth rotates on its axis. Explain to Me the concept of night and day. If you know so much, tell Me how the seasons know when to come and go." (Job 38.)

We don't do anything without the help of the Master. It's all God! We need to give Him the glory every day for giving us breath in our lungs. We must give Him the glory for every healing we experience and for every dime in our bank accounts.

God is a good God, and His handiwork is worthy to be displayed. Hallelujah!

Love Brings Peace

When we walk in obedience to God's commands, the fruit of the Spirit is manifested in our lives.

The fruit of the Spirit is love, joy, peace, longsuffering, gentleness, goodness, faith, meekness, temperance.

Galatians 5:22,23

Peace is part of the love of God. One of the most important things we have in life is peace. We can't let people rob us of it. We must protect it at all cost. Even when someone's getting on your last nerve, you cannot afford to cuss him out or remain angry. Actions like these violate your peace and hinder the will of God. The Bible states, **If any man offend not in word, the same is a perfect man, and able also to bridle the whole body** (James 3:2). However, if you do not restrain your mouth, your peace goes out the door.

When we speak without restraint, pride is the motivating factor. In essence we are saying, "Regardless of what the Word says, I'm going to say and do what I want this time." When we refuse to comply with God, that's pride. And the Bible is clear about pride: **Pride goeth before destruction, and an haughty spirit before a fall** (Prov. 6:18). So rather than put yourself in jeopardy with God, it would be wiser to respond, "Thank God I'm saved."

Love develops character in us so that we won't respond in the way pride has conditioned us to respond. Love enables us to shut our mouths, turn our heads and bless those who curse us. When we begin walking in love to this degree, we'll congratulate ourselves, saying, "I really *must* be saved, because only someone saved by God's grace could love like this!"

Love Is Not Rude

Some people try to label their rudeness as boldness. But being rude doesn't mean we're bold. It means we have no manners, no training and no love.

Even worldly people know the value of manners. "Excuse me." "I beg your pardon." "I apologize." "Yes, sir." "No, ma'am." "Thank you." "Please."

I've met rude Christians. They look good at church, but don't catch them in public! They figure that just because they've been saved for twenty years, they have the right to be rude. Or because they're "too busy," they don't have to be concerned about others. But we can never become so "spiritual" or so "busy" that we have the right to be rude to others.

The Bible says that love is not rude or unmannerly. As Christians, we should allow the personality of the Holy Spirit to manifest in our lives. He is a gentleman.

Love Is Not Self-Seeking

Love is not selfish; however, lust is. When we just want stuff for our own selfish reasons and we don't consider others, that's not real love. Real love always gives.

Everything we experience as Christians is the result of God's love for us. Jesus' crucifixion was an act of love. John 3:16 says,

But God so loved the world, that he gave his only begotten Son, that whosoever believeth in him should not perish, but have everlasting life.

God loved us so much that He *gave.* We cannot talk about love without talking about giving. Giving is serving. God loved the world to the point that it moved Him to give us His most precious gift—His Son. It moved Him to give something so awesome, so valuable, and it cost Him a great deal.

This sounds simple enough, yet few really comprehend it. We're comfortable with the idea of a powerful God. We can understand a God who desires to be served. But it's pretty tough to believe this Almighty God could love us so deeply that He would give so much. And when we accept His gracious gift of love, we should graciously share it with others.

Love Is Not Touchy, Fretful or Resentful

When we are rooted and grounded in God's love and purpose in our hearts to share it with those around us, we prevent ourselves from being touchy, fretful or resentful. Personally, when I think of these emotions, I think of children. Sometimes my girls are touchy and fretful. They shout, "Leave me alone!" "She touched me!" "Stop it!"

Ironically, it's not only my children who act this way. Adults are guilty too. They are easily offended and say things like, "She didn't speak to me. I walked right up to her and she acted as if she didn't see me."

Many of us have a lot of growing up to do. And it's going to take the love of God to get over such petty behavior. But with consistent effort, it can be done. Don't be overly concerned about the other person's behavior. Remember, if you make one step, God will do the rest.

Love Lets Go

Love does not take account of the evil done to it; it doesn't pay attention to a suffered wrong. But most Christians pay *a lot* of attention to wrongs suffered. In fact, they pay *years* of attention to them.

Offense and wrongs suffered are the devil's way of attacking our love walk and level of faith. Dwelling on those things gives him a foothold—something he has no business having!

Remember, we don't love based on how we feel. We love others because God first loved us.

And what can separate us from the love of God? Nothing! (Rom. 8:39.)

Love Covers
With Silence

6

Chapter 6

Love Covers With Silence

We should never gloat over another person's mistakes. That's not the love of God. The Bible makes this very plain in 1 Corinthians 13:6: **Love rejoiceth not in iniquity, but rejoiceth in the truth.** Instead of enjoying the fact that a brother or sister in Christ has fallen, we should be concerned that he or she gave in to the temptation in the first place. Too often we sit back and do nothing instead of trying to help the person get back up on his feet. That's a real shame.

James 5:16 says to **confess your faults one to another...that ye may be healed.** In other words, confess your struggles to a trusted friend, and allow that confession to strengthen your resolve to overcome temptation. However, few Christians apply this principle. Why? Because too many of us operate in judgement and self-righteous anger, leaving little room for mercy, compassion or help. In fact, members of the Body of Christ seem to be the first to kick you when you're down! Because of this, in an effort to avoid having our reputations smeared, most of us would rather not confess anything to anyone.

God's system is an exchange of weaknesses and strengths: The strong bear the infirmities of the weak. In real covenant friendship, we exchange weaknesses and strengths, until we eliminate the weaknesses. But we have to walk in love in order for people to trust us.

Covering Others With Love

I like this translation of 1 Corinthians 13:

It [love] *does not rejoice at injustice and unrighteousness, but rejoices when right and truth prevail.*

Love bears up under anything and everything that comes, is ever ready to believe the best of every person, its hopes are fadeless under all circumstances, and it endures everything [without weakening].

1 Corinthians 13:6,7 AMP

I've known preachers who have fallen into sin. One of them had to check himself into an institution. He was shocked to see me the first time I went to visit him. He was so sure that, like many others, I had only come to hurt him more with words of condemnation. He actually asked me to leave, but I refused. I had already predetermined that we would have communion together that day, so I found a cracker and some juice. Then I sat down with him to make a covenant agreement with him. I grabbed his face and said, "I promise to love you forever. And if you should die, I'll see to it that your wife is taken care of and that your children get a first-class education. I will not leave you, no matter what you do. I love you unconditionally."

He was so moved by the level of God's compassion—by the fact that God would actually send someone to convey His love at such a time—that he was blown away. We both cried.

I still cry every time we get together, because I think, *What if I had killed him with my words and actions? Where would he be today?* Now this man of God is whole. He made a complete recovery and is even more anointed now than he was before.

There's no greater joy than seeing people climb out of the pit of despair and press on to higher levels of spirituality. That's the way God meant it to be. However, there will always be some who say,

"Shame on those preachers! They need to get up and confess exactly what they did."

Unfortunately, most Christians are not mature enough to hear these men and women of God confess their sins. When counseling fellow ministers, I strongly suggest they tell the congregation, "I have sinned, and I'm in recovery. Please pray for me." That's all anyone needs to know.

God Doesn't Change His Mind

It's so easy to point a finger at high-profile individuals while their sins are broadcasted all over the media and ours remain hidden. But no matter how messed up some people may be, they are still equipped to continue the work God has called them to do. The Bible says, **For the gifts and calling of God are without repentance** (Rom. 11:29).

That means God doesn't change His mind about the anointing he has placed on men and women of God. That's not to say that they can sin and still have the power of God flowing freely in their lives. What it means is that, although their sins may hinder the anointing, God does not remove the anointing from their lives altogether. As a matter of fact, He restores it in even greater portions when they repent and change their ways.

Jesus' biggest challenge was not with sinners but with those in the church. It wasn't the sinners who crucified Jesus—it was the religious ones, the Pharisees and Sadducees, who convinced the Roman officials to kill Him.

When we see our brothers and sisters in sin, that is our cue to begin lifting them up in prayer. It is vital that we learn how to cover them with love and silence—keeping our mouths closed. I know certain things about people that I'll take to heaven with me, because true, committed love covers with silence.

Now, this principle may sound strange. But covering love with silence doesn't mean covering up something illegal. It simply means that we are not to expose the sin of others through gossip and backbiting. Unfortunately, some people think they have been called to do just the opposite. You may be thinking, *Brother Dollar, I'm confused! Does God want me to cover up sin or to confess it?* Scripture answers this question clearly.

Hatred stirs up contentions, but love covers all transgressions.

Proverbs 10:12 AMP

Above all things have intense and unfailing love for one another, for love covers a multitude of sins [forgives and disregards the offenses of others].

1 Peter 4:8 AMP

Walking in God's love means that you simply do not use some-one else's mistake to your advantage. Unfortunately, this scenario is altogther too common in the Body of Christ. What often happens is that somebody pours his heart out, we promise to keep it to ourselves and then we get on the telephone and tell everyone in the church what he's done.

In essence, we slice up that person's heart into tiny pieces and give them to whoever is interested in taking them. To make matters worse, we try to justify our gossip by saying, "The reason I'm telling you is that you need to know what to pray about concerning so-and-so."

Before you know it, this "prayer chain" goes around full circle and gets back to the one who poured his heart out. As a result, this brother feels rejected, condemned and worthless. Eventually he leaves the church and moves out of the protective circle of the will of God.

Be Willing To Listen

Even though we have a love relationship with the Father, every now and again it's nice to talk to someone we can see and touch—someone who can correct us, put his arms around us, say everything is going to be all right and encourage us that we're going to make it. It's for this reason that we ought to feel privileged when someone trusts us enough to say, "I need to tell you something."

However, there are those who are more concerned about their reputations than about walking in love. They don't want to have anything to do with certain people because they fear hanging around them will cause others to think poorly of them.

That's tragic. We'll never truly experience the fullness of God—His prosperity, healing, deliverance and peace—if we remain in bondage to people. We can't bring a sinner to Christ if we're too ashamed to walk down the street with him! "Well, Brother Dollar, I don't want to walk with him because he smells like alcohol, and if somebody from the church sees us, they'll think I'm drinking too." That's a poor excuse to tell God on Judgment Day.

Are You Without Sin?

God can't use us if we're thinking of ourselves more highly than we ought. What do you think the religious leaders of Israel thought when Jesus accepted a dinner invitation from a sinner? How do you think they reacted when, after bringing Jesus a woman caught in adultery, He bent down to the ground and said, **He that is without sin among you, let him first cast a stone** (John 8:7)?

In other words, check your motivation for exposing the sin of others. Do you have an intense desire to see that person delivered, or do you want more news for the grapevine? Our job as Christians is not to condemn those who fall, but to help them find the way out of the pit. When people come and ask about certain situations, just put it right back on them. You can say something like, "Oh, you want to talk about sister so-and-so? Well, let's take a look at your life first. Do you have any skeletons in your closet? It seems to me like you have too much cleaning to do before trying to expose someone else!"

Be Prudent With Your Testimony

We must also remember to be good stewards of our personal testimonies. That means we must allow God the freedom to direct us in what to share, how much information to give and whom to give it to. The Bible says in 2 Corinthians 5:17, **Therefore if any man be in Christ, he is a new creature: old things are passed away; behold, all things are become new.**

So unless the Lord prompts you to minister to others by sharing the sin of the past, leave things as they are. Sometimes what people don't know about you won't hurt them.

You see, people are not quite ready in their human nature to deal with what you used to do. For example, you may have been a prostitute or a drug addict. You may even have been an alcoholic or a homosexual. And although the blood of Jesus has wiped away the sin of the past, there are those who are not quite mature enough to handle a testimony of that magnitude. That's why it's so important that we learn how to walk in discretion and allow the Holy Spirit to lead us.

We Must Confess Our Sins

While God's love may cover sins, it exposes our own. Proverbs 28:13 says, **He that covereth his sins shall not prosper: But whoso confesseth and forsaketh them shall have mercy.**

We must confess our sins to the Father, because sin hinders our relationship with Him. However, the Bible says, **If we confess our sins, he is faithful and just to forgive us our sins, and to cleanse us from all unrighteousness** (1 John 1:9). In other words, God is bound by His Word to cleanse us of all wrong-doing when we confess it to Him. And that doesn't mean leaving things out and confessing 99.9 percent of it. For true repentance, we must confess all wrongdoing, receive God's forgiveness and learn from our mistakes. Sin will not just go away by itself.

Don't Violate the Law of Love

Unfortunately we often put God's plan in reverse. We want to use love to cover up our own wrongdoing, while exposing someone else's. We justify our actions by telling ourselves, "Oh, I'm not condemning him. I'm merely making an observation!" And then we turn around and say, "I believe the Lord will meet all of my needs for this day. Money cometh!"

You cannot violate God's principles and expect Him to work on your behalf. By doing so, you cancel out the blessings He desires to shower upon you. It's time to stop trying to take advantage of the system God has put in place. There is no easy way out of sin. However, the love of God can ease the pain that results from the unwise decisions we make. And by adhering to the law of love, we experience the fullness of God as never before.

Love That Forgets

7

Chapter 7

Love That Forgets

Unforgiveness drains power from our love walk. By refusing to let go of past hurts, we hinder God's wonder-working power in our lives and prevent His blessings from manifesting. You may be thinking, *But, Brother Dollar, I have a right not to forgive this person! You don't know what he did to me!*

That doesn't matter. If you continue to dwell on those things and then respond just as the world does, how will anyone be able to tell the difference between you and someone who doesn't know Christ? Consider what Jesus had to say about people who mistreat us:

Ye have heard that it hath been said, Thou shalt love thy neighbour, and hate thine enemy.

But I say unto you, Love your enemies, bless them that curse you, do good to them that hate you, and pray for them which despitefully use you, and persecute you; that ye may be the children of your Father which is in heaven: for he maketh his sun to rise on the evil and on the good, and sendeth rain on the just and on the unjust.

Matthew 5:43-45

Jesus' love involves more than just loving your brothers and sisters in Christ or even loving those who aren't saved. His love requires us to love our *enemies!* Jesus doesn't want us to love only when it's comfortable for us to do so, but also when it's uncomfortable. In order to be like Him, we must allow our character to be stretched and molded into His image. That means choosing to love those who oppose us or even hurt us. Now, He's not telling us to make them our best friends. But we do have to set our will to forgive them and lift them up continually before God.

That's what real love is all about. It's saying, "I'm going to do right even when someone else is doing me wrong." In doing so, you release God's anointing to correct the situation and change the hearts of all parties involved.

Take It to God

Love, like dynamite, is a powerful force that changes things. If you have problems letting go of past offenses, take them to God, the source of love, and allow Him to heal the hurt.

I once prayed for a preacher who talked about me publicly for years. When I did, God filled me with so much love for that man that I sent him a gift of $17,000. He didn't know what to do. My action caught him completely by surprise. He called me the next day, but he had a hard time putting his thoughts together to talk to me. I knew he was totally ashamed of the things he had said in the past.

When he could finally speak, he told me a story about something that had happened in a church meeting not long before. He said he had called the members of his church together in order to discuss the "heretical" teachings he had been accusing me of preaching. In the midst of the discussion, another man in the group said, "It's mighty funny that he's the only pastor in this area with the money to pay for his vision. So before we criticize him any further, let's take a good look at what he's teaching, and maybe he can help us get what we need to finance our vision."

The compassion God poured through me moved that congregation to repent! During our conversation, the preacher finally said, "I want you to forgive me for everything I've ever said about you. God showed me that I was wrong." You see, he tapped into something more powerful than hatred—the love of God! That pastor is now walking in a higher level of faith because of the awesome power of God's love.

It wouldn't have done any good for me to have hated him back. I could have retaliated, but it only would have distanced me from God and His power.

When we operate in unforgiveness, we don't hurt anyone but ourselves. Unforgiveness hinders our faith and prevents the power of God from flowing in our lives.

Let Go of Past Offenses

You can't allow those who have hurt you in the past to continue hurting you. What I mean is, every time you dwell on past hurts and offenses, you allow that person or group of people to hurt you all over again. Think about it. Do you feel better after thinking about how you were mistreated, or do you feel worse? Nine times out of ten you want to take revenge for what they did to you. The more you replay the memory, the angrier you get. And if nothing is done to resolve the issue, that anger will fester into something called bitterness.

In Ephesians 4:31-32, God commands us to get rid of bitterness. Why? Because bitterness turns into rage, and rage is often the spirit behind murder. In Matthew 5:21-22 Jesus talks about the danger of judgment faced by murderers. He goes on to say that the *same* judgment falls upon those who remain angry with another without cause. That alone should change your mind when it comes to holding ill feelings against others.

So what can you do to prevent that from happening? The first thing to do is repent. Repent for harboring those feelings for so long and remaining in a portion of offense. Then find out what God has to say about forgiveness, and make a quality decision to obey His Word in that area. By setting your will to forgive, you allow God to move on your behalf. That's why it's absolutely critical that you disconnect from the past and say, "I refuse to hate so-and-so, because I'm not going to let hatred stop me from becoming the very best that God wants me to be."

It is easier to harbor unforgiveness in your heart. You may try to ignore it or cover it up with all kinds of good deeds, but the truth is, it will always resurface. In fact, unforgiveness may be the very reason why your prayers haven't been answered. It may be that you've been hurt by an ex-spouse, an absent parent or an overbearing co-worker. And instead of resolving the issue immediately, you've allowed it to fester inside of your heart. Unfortunately, all that does is add fuel to the fire. Rather than giving those hurts to God in prayer and letting them go, you may say, "I'll forgive, but I won't forget!" However, by doing so, you forfeit the blessings and power God desires to give you.

Now we're back to the subject of partial disobedience, which we discussed in chapter 1. You obeyed the Word of God by taking your hurts to God in prayer, but you actually operated in disobedience because you wouldn't completely let go.

In clearer terms, by choosing to hold on to past offenses, you establish your own righteousness and forfeit the righteousness God has given to you through Jesus Christ. You can probably list a million reasons as to why you have the right to hate this person or that person. But the truth is that, by doing so, you are only hurting yourself.

Unleash God's Power—Forgive

When we forgive others, God forgives us. Galatians 6:7 says we reap what we sow. That's God's kingdom system—seedtime and harvest. When you sow the seeds of forgiveness, love and mercy, you reap the same harvest. Setting your will to forgive another person ushers in the power of God like never before. That's why Jesus said:

Have faith in God. For verily I say unto you, that whosoever shall say unto this mountain, Be thou removed, and be thou cast into the sea; and shall not doubt in his heart, but shall believe that those things which he saith shall come to pass; he shall have whatsoever he saith. Therefore I say unto you, What things soever ye desire, when ye pray, believe that ye receive them, and ye shall have them. And when ye stand praying, forgive, if ye have ought against any: that your Father also which is in heaven may forgive you your trespasses. But if ye do not forgive, neither will your Father which is in heaven forgive your trespasses.

Mark 11:22-26

This passage of Scripture begins with the powerful subject of faith. It advises us to maintain high levels of faith in order to remove obstacles and receive answers to our prayers. However, it concludes with a warning: "Watch out for the spirit of unforgiveness!"

What we do for others determines what God does for us. If we forgive others, He forgives us. If we do not forgive others, He cannot forgive us. It's not that He doesn't want to forgive us; it's just that God can't go back on His Word. When you sow a seed, you reap a harvest. Good seed equals good harvest. Bad seed equals bad harvest. When you sow forgiveness, you will reap the same from God. In other words, if we will, He will. If we won't, He won't.

Unforgiveness Stops Faith

The cancer of unforgiveness hinders spiritual growth. In fact, it stops you from operating by or receiving the end of your faith. Without faith, it is impossible to please God.

For therein is the righteousness of God revealed from faith to faith: as it is written, **The just shall live by faith.**

Romans 1:17

But without faith it is impossible to please him: *for he that cometh to God must believe that he is, and that he is a rewarder of them that diligently seek him.*

Hebrews 11:6

Unforgiveness is the biggest roadblock to the blessings of God. Why? Because it hinders your faith and, as a result, blocks up every area of your life: prayer, deliverance, prosperity and healing. That means your confessions of faith are useless—nothing more than idle words without forgiveness.

Unforgiveness Hinders Our Prayers

When Jesus taught His disciples to pray, He included this statement: **Forgive us our debts, as we forgive our debtors** (Matt. 6:12). After He had finished, He taught them this lesson:

For if ye forgive men their trespasses, your heavenly Father will also forgive you: but if ye forgive not men their trespasses, neither will your Father forgive your trespasses.

Matthew 6:14,15

Notice Jesus ended by talking about forgiveness, not joy, peace or the Holy Ghost. Obviously unforgiveness paralyzes not only our relationships with one another, but more importantly, our relationship with the Father.

Forgiving those who have hurt you determines the difference between success and failure in the things of God. To allow unforgiveness to fester in your heart is a slap in the face to God. Why? Because you're turning your back on the things He desires for you to have—prosperity, long life, peace, health and wisdom—for the opposite: poverty, sickness, ignorance and death. Spiritual success is not based on the number of good deeds you do annually but on how consistently you obey God.

In Matthew 18:23-35, Jesus tells of a servant who is forgiven a sizeable debt yet refuses to forgive the debt of a man who owes him money. When the servant's master discovers what he has done, the master says:

O thou wicked servant, I forgave thee all that debt, because thou desiredst me: shouldest not thou also have had compassion on thy fellowservant, even as I had pity on thee? And his lord was wroth, and delivered him to the tormentors, till he should pay all that was due unto him.

Matthew 18:32-34

Jesus concludes the story with this sobering statement:

So likewise shall my heavenly Father do also unto you, if ye from your hearts forgive not every one his brother their trespasses.

Matthew 18:35

In this parable, Jesus says the servant owed his master ten thousand talents of gold. By today's standards, that's approximately $20 million! So let's make this a little more personal. Let's say you have $20 million in your bank account. However, your cousin finds your checkbook, writes a check to himself for $20 million, cashes it and leaves you with a zero balance. What would you do? You *should* do exactly as the man in the parable—forgive the debt and let your cousin go on about his business.

Well, praise the Lord! Your cousin doesn't have to go to jail, because you're not pressing charges. However, as he's walking down the street, he meets his friend and says, "Hey! You owe me $20! What? You don't have my $20?" Then he angrily puts his hands around the man's throat and has him thrown in jail.

Now, word gets back to you about what your cousin's been up to, and it makes you mad! You just forgave him of a $20 million debt, and he throws his friend in jail for $20! So what do you do? You throw him in jail, too, until he can repay you the $20 million!

Jesus Paid Our Debt

The price that Jesus had to pay for our sins is just like that $20 million debt. The things we must forgive others for are petty compared to the price He paid for us. When God commands us to forgive one another, the debts we forgive are no greater than the $20 in the parable.

However, we often have a hard time forgiving our neighbor for walking by and not speaking to us! And now instead of dwelling on good things as we are told in Galatians 5:22-23, we dwell on the fact that this person did not speak to us. We become insecure, self-conscious and angry.

Believe it or not, our spiritual circumstances are not caused by what others do. They are the result of our failure to forgive. It's vital that we forgive, apply the blood of Jesus to our wounds and allow God to heal our hurts, instead of making excuses for where we are now.

You're Not Alone

Jesus is touched by your infirmities. (Heb. 4:15.) He knows what you've gone through, and He continuously offers you opportunities to be free of the past. His anointing empowers you to forgive so His blessings can manifest themselves in your life.

However, before He gives us His power, we must set our will to forgive those who have hurt us. Instead of saying, "I'll forgive, but I'll never forget," you must choose to say, "I completely forgive so-and-so. I will not hold to the issue. And I pray God's blessing upon his life."

Seventy Times Seven

You may be wondering, *How far do I take this forgiveness thing?* Let's see what the Bible says.

Then came Peter to him, and said, Lord, how oft shall my brother sin against me, and I forgive him? till seven times?

Jesus saith unto him, I say not unto thee, Until seven times: but, Until seventy times seven.

Matthew 18:21,22

Take heed to yourselves: If thy brother trespass against thee, rebuke him; and if he repent, forgive him. And if he trespass against thee seven times in a day, and seven times in a day turn again to thee, saying, I repent; thou shalt forgive him.

Luke 17:3,4

In Matthew, Jesus said to forgive seventy times seven. That's 490 times. In Luke, He says to forgive each day. However, that doesn't mean that you limit forgiveness to 490 times a day. Unlimited forgiveness of others means God will forgive you an unlimited number of times. Remember, God does whatever He requires us to do.

You Can Forgive

The process of forgiving may not be easy at first, but it is certainly possible to do. Jesus said, **He that believeth on me, the works that I do shall he do also; and greater works than these shall he do; because I go unto my Father** (John 14:12).

When you make a quality decision to forgive another person, the anointing power of God comes in to remove the burden and destroy the yoke that wound has placed in your life. In other words, the anointing sets you free.

That's character! It takes a true man or woman God to say in the midst of persecution, "I bless you in the name of Jesus." But the more you pray for those who have hurt you, the better you will feel. Before you know it, God's love, blessings and power will overtake you completely!

Family Love

Chapter 8

Family Love

It is important to learn how to love your family with the love of God. This can be a challenge, because many of us have at least one or two relatives who irritate us to no end. However, God requires us to love everyone—including those not-so-easy-to-get-along-with family members. The problem is, most of us don't know how to show the love of God to them. And if you've never really been taught about true, biblical love, you'll fail the love test every time.

Loving people where they are spiritually, mentally and emotionally is vitally important to any relationship. Yes, it's good to set high expectations, but they can't be so far into the stratosphere that no one can meet them. The only thing you'll be doing is fostering feelings of inadequacy in those you're trying to love. The love of God challenges those around you, but at the same time recognizes their limitations and stays committed to them anyway.

As human beings, we are extremely limited in what we can do, think or believe. However, God accepts us as we are and still chooses to stand by us and shower us with His blessings daily. True love doesn't give up on people just because they are irritating or because they make mistakes.

Love Is Willing To Change

My wife told me once, "Don't you dare tell God how much you love Him if you are not willing to change." This holds very true in all of our relationships, but especially in our families. Change is the evidence of love. In essence it says, "I'm willing to change whatever I need to change so I can line up with what God wants me to be."

One of the things that caused me to fall in love with my wife was her willingness to change. She was more willing than I was to become a better person. After awhile I had to recognize the fact that I couldn't tell her I loved her and still keep my old attitude by saying, "That's just how I am. Take me as I am, or go find somebody else." That is not the kind of attitude love portrays. That's just a demonstration of our immaturity and inability to love as God loves.

You may be thinking, *Well, I'm not changing until so-and-so changes.* That's the wrong attitude to take! Change must be sown before it can be harvested. You can't point your finger and say, "As soon as you quit acting like that, I'll change." The truth is, as soon as we quit acting like that and set our hearts and minds to change our thinking and behavior, the other person will change. It's a kingdom principle: If you sow change, you'll reap change.

We Had To Change for God

The same principle applies to our relationship with God. We have to make adjustments in our lives because of our love for Him; and because of our willingness to change, He helps us and gives us everything we need for successful Christian living.

Before coming to Christ, most of us were involved in all kinds of ungodly activities. We were full of sin, pride and rebellion. We allowed our flesh to lead our lives. However, in spite of all of that, God reached down, touched our hearts and opened our eyes to a whole new level of living. For the first time in our lives, we understood the awesome love and compassion of God. But we could not continue to say we loved Him without evidence of that love. We knew we had to be obedient to His Word and put that love into action by changing our ways of thinking and doing. That's how we demonstrate love to God—by combining actions with our words.

God Makes Adjustments for Us

God is willing to adjust His plans and methods of operation in order to make a way for us. For example, even after Adam and Eve disobeyed His command not to eat from a certain tree in the Garden of Eden, God still made a way for their sin to be atoned for. He created a system whereby the blood of sheep, goats and other animals could cover the sin of man once a year, until the final sacrifice—Jesus—came to earth.

"But, Brother Dollar! Doesn't the Bible say that God never changes?" Yes! Malachi 3:6 says, **I am the Lord, I change not.** God does not change. His Word endures forever. However, God may postpone His original plans for a time in order to bring us back into the center of His will.

Follow God's Example

If God is willing to make adjustments for us, how much more should we be willing to change and conform to His Word?

When I was a baby Christian, there were many times I thought, *I can't help how I am. It's too late for me to change!*

118

However, this is not the case. Jesus said in Matthew 19:26, **With men this is impossible, but with God all things are possible.** And Paul stated in Philippians 4:13, **I can do all things through Christ which strengtheneth me.** The time for excuses has come to an end. If you have made a quality decision to live according to the Word of God, now is the time to make whatever adjustments are necessary in your life.

But let's flip the coin for the sake of adding balance. What will happen to you if you *don't* change? Psalm 55:19 says, **God shall hear, and afflict them, even he that abideth of old…. Because they have no changes, therefore they fear not God.**

What is the fear of God? To be willing to align ourselves with His Word, no matter the cost. To fear God is to obey Him; and according to John 14:15, we can't say we love Him if we don't obey His commands.

Love Is Not Rude

Love is not rude (1 Cor. 13:5 AMP). Love is not unmannerly. This principle certainly applies to our households. We can't be rude to our family members and then come to church and pretend to be as sweet as can be. Rather than shouting orders at your kids or nagging your spouse about bills or chores, try asking them politely. Watch your tone of voice. A smile and a "please" or "thank you" go a long way toward maintaining peace.

Love Is Not Selfish

First Corinthians 13:5 (AMP) says, **Love (God's love in us) does not insist on its own rights or its own way, for it is not self-seeking.** Love is never selfish. It sets its own desires to the side for the benefit of another. Love is more concerned with how you can meet the needs of another than how you would like your needs to be met.

Love Is Not Easily Provoked

When we take our eyes off our own agendas and desires in order to serve our families, it prevents us from becoming easily angered. First Corinthians 13:5 says, [Love] **is not easily provoked...**[love] **thinketh no evil.** In other words, love is not quick to take offense. It doesn't keep scorecards of hurts and offenses.

I can identify with the way the *The Amplified Bible* explains 1 Corinthians 13:5: [Love] **is not touchy or fretful.** There are times when I am tired and irritable and I don't want anybody to talk to me. However, if I want to obey God's Word, I have to get past that irritability and bite my tongue until I've had a good night's sleep.

First Corinthians 13:5 AMP continues by saying that love is not resentful. Too many of us carry resentment around with us like a piece of luggage. The only thing this does is grow into anger, rage and bitterness, and it hinders God's blessings from manifesting in our lives.

A Loveless Home Equals a Loveless Society

A lack of love in the home always leads to a loveless society. Why? Because society is a mirror image of what's going on at home. It's the law of seedtime and harvest. For example, if you sow seeds of love into a child, you will reap a harvest of the same. That child will grow up happy, well-adjusted and well-equipped to handle the world around him. However, if seeds of anger, scorn, bitterness and hurt are sown, nine times out of ten that child will go out into the world looking for what was missing in his family.

We shouldn't be surprised when some young man joins a gang or some young girl finds an older man to sleep with. They are trying to fulfill the emptiness inside of them with outside influences—people who accept them as they are and remain committed to them no matter what. They are the products of loveless homes. Society is simply a reflection of a need for love that is not being met.

Love Disciplines

Real love disciplines and trains. And these are not things you do once in a lifetime. They're continuous. Parents should not be surprised when their children act up and misbehave. If children could make quality decisions on their own, they wouldn't need parents to train them!

Now, in my house, we don't have a democracy. I run my house God's way. Taffi and I train our children in the nurture and admonition of *the Lord.* (Eph. 6:4.) We don't ask our relatives to vote on what we do in our house. And that includes my children.

When I was a child, I never could understand why Mama or Daddy said, "We discipline you because we love you." However, as I grew older, I remembered what they said. It was their love for me that prevented me from doing things I would later regret. I thought about that love at home, and it restrained me. That's the God kind of love.

The Bible says in Proverbs 13:24, **He that spareth his rod hateth his son: but he that loveth him chasteneth him betimes.** The parents who love their children don't wait until they get old before they chasten them. Instead, they diligently discipline them from an early age. Discipline is evidence of your love for your children. You don't really love your children if you don't take the time to correct them.

Today parents get offended when you try to talk to them about their children. They don't want to discipline them, but neither do they want you to do it. I grew up in a neighborhood where everyone was allowed to correct me. My mother's neighbors used to brag about that. One time I got paddled by a lady who lived down the street from us. She paddled me and then called my mom to say, "I just whipped your son." Unbelievably, my mom said, "Thank you. Send him down here, so I can whip him again!"

Love Has Manners

My sisters and I were often punished if we failed to practice good manners. We weren't sassy. We were taught to say, "Yes, ma'am," "No, ma'am," "Yes, sir," "No, sir," "Thank you" and "Please."

Now when my own children bring their friends over to play, I tell them, "Let them know that if they can't learn manners, they don't come into the house."

That's training!

Your Children Are That Way Because of You

Most children rebel because they want to get their parents' attention. They deliberately get in trouble in order to get you to notice them. Whether you believe it or not, children want to be disciplined. They want to know that there are certain boundaries they can't cross. It assures them of your love for them. Children who rebel are the very same children who rarely hear their parents tell them, "I love you."

Children desire to be loved and appreciated. They want their problems to be just as important as an adult's. Instead of being shoved to the side, they want to hear their parents say something like, "Wow, is that what happened today?" or "That's a mighty fine smiley face on your homework, son!"

When your children give you a drawing that looks like a blob of color, you should say, "You made this for me? Oh, give me a hug. I'll put this on my desk so I can look at it every day."

Taffi is always telling me that our children are the way they are because of us. They are little mirror images of Taffi and Creflo Dollar, not Joe Christian down the street. In them we see every good and bad aspect of ourselves. But we have confidence that they are influenced by us and our love for them. We're not allowing their fragile, innocent minds to be shaped and molded by someone else. Instead, we're doing as God instructed by training them up in the way they should go.

Pray for Your Children

The Bible tells us in Ephesians 6:12 that we **wrestle not against flesh and blood, but against principalities, against powers, against the rulers of the darkness of this world, against spiritual wickedness in high places.** There are forces from the pit of hell that want to destroy our children. However, God does not want us to live in fear, wondering what will happen to them every second of their lives.

Instead of giving in to the fear the enemy strives to plant in our minds, we must seize every opportunity we have to pray for our children. Because of the world we live in and its constantly deteriorating state, we cannot afford to be traditional in prayer. Desperate times call for desperate action. That means speaking the promises of God over your life and the lives of your children daily. Here are some promises you can declare over your children every day.

And all thy children shall be taught of the Lord; and great shall be the peace of thy children.

Isaiah 54:13

Are they not all ministering spirits, sent forth to minister for them who shall be heirs of salvation?

Hebrews 1:14

The Greek word for *salvation,* is *soteria,* which means "rescue or safety; deliverance, health, salvation."[1] In other words, this verse tells us that angels have been sent forth to minister to us, because we are heirs of God's promises of protection, safety and preservation. God has sent angels to minister to and serve us and our children. That's their job.

It's vital that parents plead the blood of Jesus over their children every morning and release the angels of God to carry them safely wherever they need to go. This paralyzes the forces of darkness that threaten to destroy our families.

Praying for their protection is one way to express godly love for your family.

Now is the time to evaluate your life and pay close attention to areas that may be lacking. You may have allowed daily prayer and confession to fall by the wayside. Or you may have forgotten how to express love to the members of your family. Whatever the case may be, it's up to you to correct the situation. Don't let another day go by without showing God's love to your family. Allow Him to direct your path so that your home can be filled to the brim with God's peace and abundance.

The Father's Love

Chapter 9

The Father's Love

God earnestly desires for us to know how to love one another. But in order to do this, we must first have a good understanding of His love for us and the ways in which He desires for us to love Him in return. In everything, God gives us an example to follow, whether it's in relationships, character or servanthood. Paul tells us in Ephesians 5:1 to be imitators of Christ as dearly loved children. Children mimic what they see and hear others doing. When we imitate God—especially in how well we love one another—we show the world that we truly belong to Him.

God loves us with an unconditional, everlasting love. There's nothing we can do to stop Him from loving us. This was made evident in that "while we were still sinners, Christ died for us." (Rom. 5:8.) The Bible also tells us in 1 John 4:19 that we love God because He first loved us. By sowing seeds of love into our lives, God is able to reap the harvest of that love through our obedience to Him.

God's love is amazing because it transcends all barriers and is based on a commitment to His Word. For hundreds of years mankind was promised a Messiah who would arrive one day to die for man and rescue him from the hand of sin and death. Just consider for a moment how great that love is! It's a love that is in hot pursuit of you. It's trying to run you over!

Be Filled With His Fullness

The Bible tells us in Ephesians 3:19, [I pray that you may] **know the love of Christ, which passeth knowledge, that ye might be filled with all the fulness of God.** Love is the avenue to being filled with everything God has to offer—His grace, power, wisdom and anointing. The only way to receive these things is to have an intimate knowledge of Christ's love. How? By reading and studying His Word on a daily basis. Fellowship with Him is the key to receiving all He has to offer.

However, you cannot comprehend God's love with your natural mind. To put it simply, it just can't be done. Revelation knowledge—supernatural understanding—is needed in order for you to grasp how great God's love really is.

Revelation is comprehension imparted into our spirits from the Holy Spirit and then transmitted to our minds. In other words, it's understanding that moves from the heart to the head. For example, before you became born again, someone told you how to get to heaven. You knew (head knowledge) that Jesus was the only way. However, the Holy Spirit illuminated that knowledge by revealing your need for Christ (revelation knowledge), and for the first time ever you became aware of the sinful state you were in. As a result of that supernatural understanding, you accepted Christ as Lord and Savior.

The same principle applies to God's love. You can study it until you're blue in the face; however, unless the Spirit of God reveals the importance of love and the greatness of God's love for you, you will not be able to experience the fullness of God. That's why it's vitally important that we ask and believe for revelation. We need to ask the Holy Spirit to speak to us through illustrations, examples and any other way, so that we can understand how deep God's love is.

Now, the only way for you to receive revelation like that is by maintaining your personal relationship with the Holy Spirit. There is no other way. Spending time with God consistently and on a daily basis opens the door for Him to speak to your heart. And not only that, but time spent with God equals more of His charac-ter deposited in us. Think about it. The Bible tells us in Exodus

34:34-35 that Moses had to cover his face after spending time with God. Why? Because the glory of God was all over him. It's impossible to spend time with God and not be affected in some way. That's when the world takes notice of who He is and who we are.

God's Love Is Tough

God's love is marked by discipline. In other words, His love for us is not measured by how much grace He pours out on us but by His correction. Paul mentioned this fact in Hebrews 12:5-10 AMP:

And have you [completely] forgotten the divine word of appeal and encouragement in which you are reasoned with and addressed as sons? My son, do not think lightly or scorn to submit to the correction and discipline of the Lord, nor lose courage and give up and faint when you are reproved or corrected by Him; for the Lord corrects and disciplines everyone whom He loves, and He punishes, even scourges, every son whom He accepts and welcomes to His heart and cherishes. You must submit to and endure [correction] for discipline; God is dealing with you as with sons.

For what son is there whom his father does not [thus] train and correct and discipline? Now if you are exempt from correction and left without discipline in which all [of God's children] share, then you are illegitimate offspring and not true sons [at all]. [Prov. 3:11,12.] *Moreover, we have had earthly fathers who disciplined us and we yielded [to them] and respected [them for training us]. Shall we not much more cheerfully submit to the Father of spirits and so [truly] live? For [our earthly fathers] disciplined us for only a short period of time and chastised us as seemed proper and good to them; but He disciplines us for our certain good, that we may become sharers in His own holiness.*

Now look at verse 5 in the *King James Version*.

And ye have forgotten the exhortation which speaketh unto you as unto children, My son, despise not thou the chastening of the Lord, nor faint when thou art rebuked of Him.

Hebrews 12:5

Most of us look for the side of love that helps us feel good about ourselves. However, according to these passages, the true proof of love is in a person's honesty. In other words, he loves you enough to tell you when you are wrong. That doesn't always give us warm, fuzzy feelings, but it helps us in the long run. If someone tells you he loves you and then lets you go on doing the wrong thing, he is lying.

Discipline shapes character. Just as a parent corrects a child in order to train him properly, so likewise our heavenly Father disciplines us for our own good. He desires for us to live victoriously in this world and to experience the magnitude of His blessings; however, that's impossible to do if we are still spiritual babes, unable to handle everything He gives to us.

It's important that we not frown on God's discipline. He's not some giant god who wants to ruin all your fun. In fact, John 10:10 says that Jesus came to give us abundant life. That doesn't sound horrible to me! God disciplines us so that we can become more like Him in everything we do. That's the only way the lost will come to know Him. And it also shows us how much He truly cares for us. I mean, He could just let us get in trouble and not lift a hand to help. But God is not like that. He wants the best for us, and discipline is a way of ensuring that we get His best. That's why Proverbs 3:11-12 says,

My son, despise not the chastening of the Lord; neither be weary of his correction: for whom the Lord loveth he correcteth; even as a father the son in whom he delighteth.

Jesus said the same thing in Revelation 3:19: **As many as I love, I rebuke and chasten: be zealous therefore, and repent.** In other words, "Don't get upset at Me if I correct you about something. I only discipline those I love. So repent, and change your heart, mind and direction!"

He Is in Love With Us

God is in love with us. And because of that love, He corrects us and shows us the way we should go. As we spend time in His presence daily, love is deposited in our hearts and stirred up by the Holy Spirit. As a result, we are strengthened in our inner man to share God's love with those around us.

It's impossible to dwell in God's presence and not be affected by it. It's in that place of prayer that we are equipped to meet the needs of the world around us. We can't do anything on our own strength and in our own love. Human love is conditional and tires easily, while God's love is unconditional and everlasting. It ushers in the anointing of God and challenges us to operate on a higher level of spirituality. God's love is the ultimate source of power. And with His love as the motivating factor behind all we do, nothing will be impossible for us.

Love Conquers All

10

Chapter 10

Love Conquers All

Before you can walk in love on a consistent basis, you must first understand its source. The Bible tells us in 1 John 4:8 that God is love. In other words, He is the source, the author, of love. Everything you could ever need or want is in that source—power, prosperity, healing and forgiveness. But it's only by tapping into and staying plugged into that source that God is able to pour these blessings out upon your life.

So how do you tap into the source of love? Through intimate, daily contact with the Father. In other words, you must establish and maintain a relationship with God. And that doesn't mean a one-sided relationship, with God doing all the work. No, you must be willing to take time out of your day to talk with Him and study His Word. A love relationship only works when both parties involved put forth the effort to maintain it. The more time you spend with God, the more His love will flow through you, and the more you become like Him in everything you do.

No More Childish Games

God's love is mature. That means it does not exhibit childish characteristics such as jealousy, envy and selfishness. Look at Paul's conclusion to 1 Corinthians 13.

But when the complete and perfect comes, the incomplete and imperfect will vanish away—become antiquated, void, and superseded.

When I was a child, I talked like a child, I thought like a child, I reasoned like a child; now that I have become a man, I am done with childish ways and have put them aside.

1 Corinthians 13:10,11 AMP

When you rebel against God's love, you are rebelling against spiritual maturity. Only a child would hold a grudge or disrespect another person. Children do these things because they're children—they don't know any better; however, adults are without excuse. Examine yourself. If you see any areas of your life in which you are doing the opposite of what Paul describes love to be in 1 Corinthians 13, repent! Make a quality decision to walk in the maturity of God's love. Meditate on His Word, and allow it to transform your life.

Does He Know You?

We must get to know our heavenly Father. It's not enough to come to church once a week or read your Bible every so often. Part-time Christianity does not work. We have been called to a higher level of existence. God desires for us to live with Him forever in heaven. But will He know you when you get to the gate?

Many will say to me in that day, Lord, Lord, have we not prophesied in thy name? and in thy name have cast out devils? and in thy name done many wonderful works? And then will I profess unto them, I never knew you: depart from me, ye that work iniquity.

Matthew 7:22,23

God says He never knew any of these people, although they were able to prophesy, heal and deliver others. I often tell my congregation that there will be a lot of surprises when we get to heaven. Some of the people we thought would be there, won't be. Ironic, isn't it?

God wants a close relationship with you right now. Just as you do with a best friend or a spouse, God wants you to consult Him daily on matters that are important to you. He wants you to value your relationship with Him to the point that He becomes the first and last One you talk to each day.

In Genesis 3:8-11 we find God walking through the Garden of Eden looking for Adam and Eve. You see, God's original plan was designed around having an intimate relationship with us. He was literally present with man in the beginning. And although today you may not see Him in the physical sense, He is always present. He's simply waiting on you to show up.

Relationship Before Ministry

We should not let anything get in the way of our time with God—including ministry. Most of us are busy serving in our local churches and working unto the Lord; however, that is no substitute for a relationship with God. Martha and Mary had very different views about this subject.

Now it came to pass, as they went, that he entered into a certain village: and a certain woman named Martha received him into her house. And she had a sister called Mary, which also sat at Jesus' feet, and heard his word. But Martha was cumbered about much serving, and came to him, and said, Lord, dost thou not care that my sister hath left me to serve alone? bid her therefore that she help me.

And Jesus answered and said unto her, Martha, Martha, thou art careful and troubled about many things: But one thing is needful: and Mary hath chosen that good part, which shall not be taken away from her.

Luke 10:38-42

Martha was busy serving guests while Mary, undistracted, sat at Jesus' feet and listened to everything He said. When Martha saw this, she asked Jesus to require that Mary get up and help her. But instead, Jesus gently rebuked her for placing more value on service than on relationship.

What happens when we become distracted and overly occupied by our service to God? We spend less time with Him, which cuts into our supply of His love, power, abundance and wisdom. In other words, our batteries become drained because we begin running or living on our own power instead of His. That's when our flesh (our desires and agendas) get in the way of God's will and purpose for our lives. Before we know it, we're back to square one.

However, by maintaining our relationship with God, we remain plugged in to the ultimate and most reliable source of power. It is at those times that we are able to handle anything that comes our way. I believe that if Martha had joined her sister as she sat at Jesus' feet, wisdom would have directed her to set up a buffet line at which everyone could serve himself!

We must not allow our service to distract us from being with God. Service does not determine how much we love God—our obedience does. Service is just another avenue whereby we can express love for God. Jesus told Martha to stop putting her service before her obedience: **"Martha, Martha, you are anxious and you're troubled about many things; there is need of only one thing, and Mary hath chosen that good part..."** (vv. 41,42 NKJV). It is only by spending time with God that we can be effective in serving and loving Him. The most anointed men and women in the world talk to God constantly. They sit at His feet and listen to every word.

If you desire to walk in the God kind of love, make a quality decision to maintain your relationship with Him. It's only by dwelling in His presence that you will find everything you need to live a prosperous, happy and successful life. Discover what it means to be a true reflection of His love, and make an eternal mark in the lives of millions.

Prayers and Confessions

Prayers and Confessions

To Walk in Love

PRAYER: Father, please forgive me for not loving as I should. Your Word says that I am made in Your image; therefore it is my desire to love as You do. Right now I tap into the anointing to change, which is made available to me through Your love. I pray that the atmosphere of my life, my home, my church and my place of work will change as a result of Your love demonstrated through me. Let it begin today. In Jesus' name I pray. Amen.

CONFESSION: In the name of Jesus, I decide right now to accept my responsibility in this walk of love. I love you, Lord, and the evidence of my love is the love I show to others. I receive Your power, Your anointing and all that comes as a result of my obedience to walk in love. I will even demonstrate love to my enemies. I open myself up to this love walk. Change me, rearrange me and make me new again. I thank You, God, that I will not miss the very best that You have for me. I won't just wear a Christian label, but I will live as a Christian as well. I believe that I receive right now the faith to walk in love, in Jesus' name.

To Walk in Forgiveness

PRAYER: Father, I make a quality decision to forgive. Your Word says in 1 John 1:9 that when I repent, You are faithful and just to forgive me and cleanse me of my sin. I will not allow unforgiveness to block my blessings, neither will it prevent me from loving at all times. (Prov. 17:17.) Right now I speak to the mountain of unforgiveness, and I say, "Be removed from my life forever, in Jesus' name." (Matt. 21:21.) Amen.

CONFESSION: In the name of Jesus, I will sow forgiveness and therefore reap forgiveness. I declare that I will not walk in unforgiveness another day in my life. By the confession of my mouth, I renounce unforgiveness. And in the name of Jesus, I set my will to forgive. I am covered by the blood.

I declare my freedom from the spirits that torment me. I declare today that, by the Spirit of God, every area of my life that has been bound by the spirit of unforgiveness is set free. Whom the Son sets free is free indeed. (John 8:36.) Therefore, every demonic force, every tormentor, I command you now, leave me! Leave my household! Leave my children! Leave my family! Be gone!

As the redeemed of the Lord, I declare now that whatever I say is so. (Ps. 107:2.) I say I'm free, and it's so. I say I walk in forgiveness, and it's so. Right now, I release every individual I've held ill feelings against. I roll all of my cares concerning them over on You, Lord God, and I'm free from them. (1 Peter 5:7.)

Now I fully expect a hundredfold return of everything that I've missed as a result of my unforgiveness. In the name of Jesus, I call the power back. I call the anointing back. I call the prosperity back. I call the deliverance back. In Jesus' name, I am totally restored and completely free!

To Walk in the Prosperity Ignited by Love

PRAYER: Lord, I pray for an increase of anointing, love and compassion. I know that promotion comes from You (Ps. 75:6,7), and I know that You are a rewarder of those who diligently seek You. (Heb. 11:6.) Because of Your favor, Lord, I expect miraculous increase in every area of my life. And I am 1000 times better from this moment on. (Deut. 1:11.) In Jesus' name. Amen.

CONFESSION: In the name of Jesus, I am rooted and grounded in the love of God. I decide today that I live and walk in love. My faith will increase. My anointing will increase. My power will increase. My prosperity will increase—because my love has increased in the name of Jesus.

Prayer for the Family

PRAYER: In the name of Jesus, I loose the spirit of love upon my family. We will sow love into each other like never before through kind words and actions. We purpose to love through difficult times and disappointments. We will cover each other in prayer daily and focus on the best in each other. I cast out unforgiveness, strife and bitterness, and I pray that each of us will learn to love as You so graciously love us. In Jesus' name. Amen.

Prayer for Children's Safety

PRAYER: I command angels to go forth now in the name of Jesus and prepare safety this day for my children. They will leave my house safely, and they will return safely. Because faith works by love, I purpose to love my children as You love them, seeing the best in them and loving them unconditionally. Your Word promises me that if I train them in the way they should go, when they are old they will not depart from Your teachings. (Prov. 22:6.) I declare it is so now, in Jesus' name. Amen.

CONFESSION: Great is the peace of my children. (Isa. 54:13.) I declare, in the name of Jesus, that no weapon formed by the devil will prosper against my children. (Isa. 54:17.)

I declare, in the name of Jesus, that angels go forth and serve my children today, providing them with safety, protection and preservation. My children have long life, and I declare that You will honor every promise found in Your Word concerning them.

In the name of Jesus, I plead the blood and settle it right now that no threat of harm, tragedy or death can enter my household! I declare it with my mouth. I make it my confession, and it is so now, in Jesus' name. Praise God! Hallelujah!

To Minister Godly Love

PRAYER: In the name of Jesus, I declare the love of God over my life as I receive His corrections, His discipline and His instruction. I will no longer function as an average Christian, but I will excel in love. I commit my ways to You, Lord God, and You will do exceedingly, abundantly above all I can ever ask or think. (Eph. 3:20.)

CONFESSION: Greater is He who is in me than he who is in the world. (1 John 4:4.) I challenge myself to make an eternal mark in the lives of people. I challenge myself to walk in a greater degree of love. I challenge myself to move instantly when I hear the voice of the Holy Ghost.

I make a decision now to be prepared to do every good work. I am anointed and appointed, and I will edify the Body of Christ. I will do the work of the ministry.

I declare, in the name of Jesus, I will not dwell in the land of complacency. I will come out of my comfort zone. I press in to reach the prize of the high calling (Phil. 3:14), which is in the Anointed One, who is in me. (1 John 2:27.)

I walk in the favor of God and in the comfort of the the Holy Ghost. I am the servant of the Almighty God!

To Increase Maturity

PRAYER: In the name of Jesus, I decide today not to act as a child any longer. I am spiritually mature. I put away childish things. (1 Cor. 13:11.) I practice the love walk of God in order for God to train me. I declare that I am an overcomer. (1 John 2:14.) I have overcome my past, and I will not be defeated by unforgiveness, envy, jealousy or resentment. Thank You, Father, for the power You have made available to me through Christ Jesus. (Phil. 4:13.) Amen.

CONFESSION: In the name of Jesus, and by the power of the Holy Ghost, I will give God the glory for every good thing that happens in my life. I will not be a useless nobody. (1 Cor. 13:2 AMP.) I am more than a conqueror! My faith is rising! My joy is rising! And in the mighty name of Jesus, I am walking in love!

Commitment To Spend Time With God

PRAYER: Father, in the name of Jesus, I make a quality decision to develop and diligently cultivate an individual love relationship with You. I will not allow my good works alone to communicate my love to You. I will seek the needful thing, which is the Word of God. I will not only be a hearer of the Word, but a doer also (James 1:23) because I love You. I commit to spending more time with You, so that I may know Your voice (John 10:4,5) and do what You instruct me to do.

CONFESSION: I declare now that I will spend time with the Father in prayer and in study of the Word of God. I will practice the presence of God because I love Him. I hear His voice and obey His Word because I love Him. (John 14:15.) Because I practice His presence, I will continually grow in my love for Him and for others.

Endnotes

Chapter 4

[1]Tindley, Charles Albert.

[2]Vine, s.v. "bless," Vol. 1, pp. 132-133.

Chapter 5

[1]Strong, "Greek," entry #5281, p. 74.

[2]Vine, s.v. "worketh," Vol. 4, pp. 231-232

Chapter 9

[1]Strong, "Greek," entry #4991, p. 70.

References

Strong, James. *Strong's Exhaustive Concordance of the Bible.* "Hebrew and Chaldee Dictionary," "Greek Dictionary of the New Testament." Nashville: Abingdon, 1890.

Tindley, Charles Albert. "Leave It There." *Hymns of Faith.* Carol Streams: Tabernacle Publishing, 1944.

Vine, W.E. *Expository Dictionary of New Testament Words.* Old Tappan: Fleming H. Revell, 1940.

About the Author

Dr. Creflo A. Dollar Jr. is the pastor and founder of World Changers Church International, a nondenominational, Word of Faith church located in College Park, Georgia. God has given him the awesome task to teach the Word of God with simplicity and understanding throughout the world.

World Changers Ministries began in 1986 with eight members, who met in a school cafeteria. Today, membership has increased to more than 20,000, and services are held in the spectacular World Dome. World Changers Ministries is also an international ministry with offices in the United Kingdom, Australia and the Republic of South Africa.

An anointed teacher and international conference speaker, Dr. Dollar can be seen and heard worldwide on the *Changing Your World* broadcast via television and radio. He is the father of five—Gregory, Jeremy, Jordan, Alexandria and Lauren Grace—and he is married to his partner in the ministry, Taffi L. Dollar. Together they are setting the standard for excellence in ministry and making an eternal mark among millions!

To contact Dr. Creflo A. Dollar Jr.,
write:

Creflo Dollar Ministries
P. O. Box 490124
College Park, Georgia 30349

*Please include your prayer requests
and comments when you write.*

Other Books by Creflo A. Dollar Jr.

The Color of Love—
Understanding God's Answer to Racism, Separation and Division
Answers Awaiting in the Presence of God
Uprooting the Spirit of Fear
Total Life Prosperity
The Anointing To Live
Exposing the Spirit of Competitive Jealousy
How To Trouble Your Trouble
Having Faith for Mysteries
S.O.S.—Help! My Flesh Needs Discipline
The Covenant Connector
The Miracle of Debt Release
How To Get Out of Debt God's Way
How To Obtain Healing
El Shaddai: Making a Demand on God's Supply
Jesus Is Our Jubilee

Available from your local bookstore.

HARRISON HOUSE

Tulsa, Oklahoma 74153

The Harrison House Vision

Proclaiming the truth and the power
Of the Gospel of Jesus Christ
With excellence;

Challenging Christians to
Live victoriously,
Grow spiritually,
Know God intimately.